M000118553

An amazing story of God's grace, mercy and love, and [the Penzes'] rock-solid discipleship, determination and faithfulness in following Christ's call to a ministry that seemed totally impossible.

Bob McDowell

Executive Director Emeritus, Warm Beach Camp and Conference Center

---

A thrilling account of God working in the hearts and lives of the Native Peoples of Western Alaska's Y-K Delta region.

Gordon Bakke

Missionary pilot; former director, Missionary Aviation Training Academy

---

In the face of overwhelming challenges, God's grace performs amazing transformation and redeems even in the most difficult circumstances.

John Rodkey

Faculty member, Westmont College; pilot at Kako

I continue to be amazed at the dedication of these folks in a very difficult place to work and under trying circumstances.

Sylvia Stewart

Author; retired missionary to Africa

I had no idea there were even any missionaries in the Far North. Truly, God's people are everywhere. [This book] certainly made me more aware of his love and people who serve him so faithfully without any fanfare.

Carolyn Meagher

Author

Vera Penz gave me my greatest earthly treasure [when I married] her daughter Debbie in 1978. She [has been] a tribute to God's grace and faithfulness as she steadfastly ministered to the native peoples of Alaska for over 60 years...I hope as you read her story, it will bless you also.

Mark Holland, MD

Dave and Vera Penz...gave their all to make a difference and give hope to many who live in rural bush Alaska.

Bill Ayers
Board Member, Kako Retreat Center

Praising God for faithfulness Phil 1:6

Vera Penz

LIVING GOLD

The Story of Dave and Vera Penz at Kako, Alaska

Joan Rawlins Husby

Blessings to you!

Joan Rawlins Husby

RainSong Press

Living Gold: The Story of Dave and Vera Penz at Kako, Alaska

Published by RainSong Press
Copyright © 2018 by Joan Rawlins Husby

Cover design by Lynnette Bonner of Indie Cover Design
  Cover image credit: Kako Retreat Center
Book interior design by Jon Stewart of Stewart Design

ISBN: 0-9821681-2-8

CONTENTS

The cross on Kako's mountain with camp buildings and airstrip below
Credit: Joan Husby

Vera Kelley Penz and David Penz
Credit: Vera Penz

Vera, Debbie, and Al Kelley at their first home in Copper Center, AK, built by Vince Joy. Cold weather set in before he could add the last tier of logs, hence the low door.
Credit: Vera Penz

The Penz family in 1968: David and Janet with
Jeanne and Valerie (back), Diane and Jonathan
Credit: Jeanne Rodkey

ACKNOWLEDGEMENTS

When I met widowed missionary Vera Kelley in 1965 at Glennallen, Alaska, and heard her story, I thought, *This needs to be in a book.*

When she married Dave Penz in 1988 and moved to the Yukon-Kuskokwim Delta to help him build a retreat center for Native people at a working gold mine called Kako, I followed their adventures with great interest. Not until 2011 did they decide the time had come to get their story on paper. I felt honored to say yes to the task.

The biggest challenge in gathering information—Kako's remote wilderness location—was overcome in August 2013 when the Penzes invited my husband and me to visit Kako Retreat Center during the annual Ladies' Berry Picking Retreat. We accepted with delight and immersed ourselves in life at Kako, getting to know the staff and the people who came for the retreat. We also dealt with everyday Alaskan challenges, such as making do with what's on hand.

As Dave told tales and answered questions, I scribbled notes like mad.

Vera and her daughter Debbie Holland dug out prayer letters and other documents covering Vera's earlier ministries and her work with Dave at Kako.

Dave's daughter Jeanne Rodkey shared the teachings of her late mother, Janet Penz, about living the Christian life. She gave me insights into her mom and dad's early lives in Alaska.

Jeanne's husband, John, part of Kako's camping ministry since his youth, was our pilot. He also shared stories and checked facts.

Many thanks to all the family members for their valuable input into this book, and especially to Dave's son, Jonathan Penz, now Kako's director. Because he'd been his father's right-hand man since childhood, Jonathan has brought a great deal of knowledge and expertise to the directorship. His explanations and fact checking have added greatly to the interest and accuracy of the narrative.

I thank the village women who shared memories of Dave, Vera, and Jan, as well as memories of Ed and Joyce Hooley, the schoolteachers who first envisioned a retreat center at Kako. These women added to my understanding of life in the bush.

Thanks to the woman who explained how young villagers are using debit cards and the Internet to order illicit drugs delivered right to their villages, and for her encouraging the parents to fight back.

John and Becky Erickson and Bill and Brenda Johnson represent the many volunteer workers and staff members who give of their time and energy to keep Kako running.

My thanks to Interact missionary friends Dave and Kay Henry for some of the stories in the book. They share with the Penzes a deep love for Native people.

Gordon Bakke of MATA (Missionary Aviation Training Academy), in Arlington, Washington, and his wife, Elaine, both read the manuscript and offered additional information and corrections, as well as photos from seven years of flying at Kako. Jeanne and John Rodkey shared family photos, as did Vera and Debbie.

I'm immensely grateful for interest, encouragement, and editing from the greatest group of writers' helpers ever: Diana Savage, Agnes Lawless Weaver, Sylvia Stewart, Ginger Kauffman, and the late Carolyn Meagher and Marjorie Sell Stewart.

Also reading the manuscript and offering encouragement and suggestions were Bob and Yvonne McDowell, the Penzes' friends (Bob is Executive Director Emeritus of Warm Beach Camp at Stanwood, Washington), and Bob's sister Lenora Spears and her husband Don.

My husband, Hank Husby, has been my constant encourager, helper, and idea man.

Many thanks to my competent, patient, and hardworking editor, Diana Savage (dianasavage.com), to Jon Stewart for making the layout look good (stewartdesign.studio), and to Lynnette Bonner for the cover design (indiecoverdesign.com).

Most of all, I thank Dave and Vera Penz for living this story with integrity, perseverance and much love for a people largely ignored but immensely valued in God's sight.

My gratitude to all who are Kako Retreat Center's "living gold." If I have misremembered someone's contribution or been less than accurate anywhere in this account, I ask for your indulgence. God bless all who have had a part in this story.

Living Gold is dedicated to the hundreds of people over the years who have given money, talent, time, or prayer to bring God's love to the people of the Yukon-Kuskokwim Delta.

LIVING GOLD

The Story of Dave and Vera Penz at Kako, Alaska

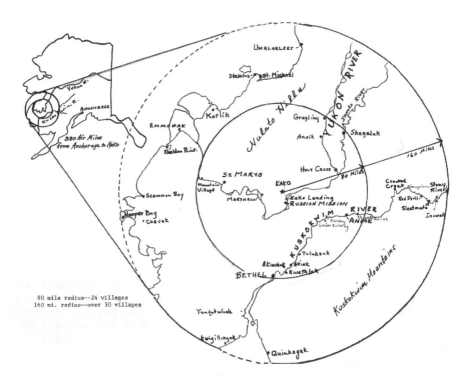

Kako's Location on the Yukon-Kuskokwim Delta

INTRODUCTION
Kako Retreat Center

Our Cessna 182 skimmed the rounded hills rimming Alaska's Yukon-Kuskokwim (Y-K) Delta. The last road connecting us to urban civilization lay behind us, 400 miles to the southeast.

Hank and I peered down through rain-splattered windows at streams twisting across boggy tundra. The wilderness seemed empty of life, except for a pair of tundra swans—only white dots in our view—and an occasional beaver lodge beside one of the innumerable ponds. We swooped over the mighty Yukon, North America's third-longest river, and a few miles farther on, descended to treetop level.

The plane touched down on a dirt airstrip, taxied past sheds and mining machinery, and stopped near several shop buildings. A few homes lined the runway, and more homes and camping cabins marched up the hill behind them. We had arrived at Kako Retreat Center (KRC).

Our pilot, John Rodkey, cut the Cessna's engine. In the sudden silence, we heard the growl of a motor approaching. John helped us out as his father- and mother-in-law, Dave and Vera Penz, pulled up on a four-wheeler. We ducked under the plane's wing, out of the rain, to be greeted warmly by the Penzes, founders and directors of the center.

They and a number of volunteer helpers were preparing for the 2013 Ladies' Berry Picking Retreat that included times of worship, teaching, and fellowship, like any women's retreat in the rest of the

US, but also with some uniquely Alaskan features. Native women from surrounding villages looked forward to climbing Kako's "mountain" in search of blueberries and crowberries to take home with them. They also enjoyed visiting with far-flung friends they seldom saw otherwise. We had come to assist in any way we could.

John and his brother-in-law, Jonathan Penz, also a bush pilot, would be transporting more than 40 women from 11 of the 56 Yupik Eskimo[1] villages within Kako's circle of influence. While flying the participants back and forth, their two small planes would log about 3,000 nautical miles.

Dave Penz, 79, had begun directing the building and operation of Kako Retreat Center more than 25 years earlier. From the center's 1980s origin in a few old cabins at a former gold mine, to today's self-contained complex, Dave's God-given vision continued to expand.

His finger was on the pulse of the whole operation: overseeing projects; building relationships with those needing spiritual assistance, as well as with those who could help further the work at Kako; and making sure that equipment and buildings stayed in repair. He was largely responsible for imagining the possibilities of Kako's outreach and planning for the needs and expansion of ministry. That ministry included not only summer camps for kids and teens, but also retreats and seminars for village men, women, and families, as well as for village teachers and other groups.

Vera handled correspondence and bookkeeping, wrote receipts for contributions, and published end-of-year photo letters. She organized schedules for those coming to and going from Kako. She cared for the house, cooked, and helped to supervise the center's

---

1   We realize that *Eskimo* is considered by some to be an offensive term these days. However, according to the Alaska Native Language Center, most Alaskans continue to accept the name *Eskimo*, particularly because *Inuit*, sometimes claimed to be a preferred term, refers only to the Inupiat of northern Alaska, the Inuit of Canada, and the Kalaallit of Greenland, and it is not a word in the Yupik languages of Alaska and Siberia. Therefore, this book will continue to use the traditional term, where appropriate.

housekeeping chores. She willingly interrupted her work when someone needed to talk. She also provided piano music whenever needed.

Hank and I were privileged to be part of the activities at Kako for a week. We watched the Penzes and the other staff at work, grew to love the village people, and saw the desperate need for hope in Jesus. We went up the mountain, along with the women who came for the retreat, to pick Alaska's delicious wild blueberries.

We were overwhelmed by the vast, beautiful landscape of mountains, valleys, and tundra. Tears ran down Hank's face as he leaned on his walking stick and gazed out over the retreat center below us to horizons hiding thousands of hearts without the gospel. Thinking of future possibilities for Kako's work, he said, "I feel like Moses looking into the Promised Land."

Kako is a continuing miracle in the wilderness. It's been built step by step with perseverance, faith in God, and the prayers and contributions of God's people—and by a generous helping of large and small miracles along the way.

This book tells the story of Kako Retreat Center, the people it serves, and Dave and Vera Penz, whom God honored with the vision and the gifts to set it all in motion.

Al Kelley with Sunday School children at Ellamar
Credit: Vera Penz

The Kelley family at their schoolhouse home in Ellamar
Credit: Vera Penz

PROLOGUE
Trouble on Prince William Sound

November 7, 1956

Al and Vera Kelley's recently acquired boat, *Evangel*, a converted 30-foot fishing vessel, chugged around the curve of land that sheltered Ellamar, Alaska, the tiny community where they lived.

As they headed across Prince William Sound, wind swooping off the Columbia Glacier hit them full force. They knew the weather forecast wasn't good, but Al thought they could turn around and go back if necessary. When whitecaps became churning swells that rolled the boat from one side to the other, Al increased power to the engine. He tried to steer in a straight line toward their destination, Valdez, but a fast-moving November storm bore down upon them. Needles of rain became slashing sleet and snow.

Vera tucked blankets around three-year-old Debbie and six-month-old Tommy where they napped on the bunk below decks. She looked up as her husband called down to her, "Sorry, Vera. We're not going to make it to the meeting this month. I'm turning around before the storm gets worse."

She nodded regretfully and sat on the bunk to keep the children from being thrown onto the floor as the old boat bucked and tossed. Al's Native helper, teenaged Jim Paulson, had been overjoyed at the chance to get away from his village. She hated to see him disappointed. She and Al had planned to see their fellow workers at the monthly Central Alaskan Missions meeting in Glennallen. In 1956, being the first Protestant missionaries to Ellamar and nearby Tatitlek was not easy. The Kelleys needed the encouragement of others who understood the challenges.

Vera heard the engine strain as Al turned the wheel. Suddenly all went silent except for the wind's howl and the creak and groan of the boat. The engine had quit! House-sized waves slammed against the side. Water sloshed across the deck.

Al guided the boat as close to the shore as possible, then he and Jim threw out the anchors. The anchors didn't do much to stabilize the boat, but at least they kept the vessel from blowing onto the rocks. The two worked frantically on the engine, but they couldn't get a spark. The magnetos on those heavy cast-iron engines were known for falling apart, and they figured that's what had happened.

The children woke and began to whimper. As Vera cared for them, she fought seasickness.

Finally Al came below deck. "We can't get it started," he said. "I think I should take the skiff we borrowed and go back to Tatitlek for help."

Vera didn't like the idea but could suggest nothing better. *Besides*, she thought, *Al is a big, strong man. If anyone can make it safely, he can.* She felt confident that the Lord would take him safely to someone who could help. He kissed the children and told them he'd be back soon, then he folded Vera in his arms. "God, watch over this family," he prayed. Vera remembered Al's earlier prayer that morning as they'd set out, that God would be glorified on this trip. She knew that prayer would be answered, but how?

With Jim's help, Al launched the eight-foot skiff. It had a 25 horsepower kicker, much too heavy for such a small boat. When Al got in, the skiff overturned, throwing him into the icy water.

Jim lunged for Al's arms and helped him back into the *Evangel*. They righted the skiff, but the kicker was gone. Al changed into dry clothes. He got into the skiff again and started rowing toward a point of land, struggling to crest the huge swells. Through the storm, Vera and Jim strained to keep the little boat in view, but flying spray and slanting snow quickly hid it from sight. They only hoped the water behind the point would be quieter and help would come soon.

CHAPTER 1
Called to the 49th State

A Happy Surprise

"I don't know whether to be pleased or dismayed!" Mae Johnson told her husband when she found herself pregnant again at the age of 40.

In 1930, at the height of the Great Depression, Jim Johnson struggled to hold on to his Oceanside masonry business on Long Island in New York state. They already had a blended family of three children. Nettie, 16, had been only six when her widowed father married Mae. Now 10-year-old Mary and two-year-old Jim completed the family. The Johnsons loved God and lived their faith. But could they support another child in these uncertain times?

Mae went to a private hospital for the delivery of her fourth child. While the doctor was attending to newborn Vera, the nurse tried to get his attention. "Another one is coming!"

Dr. Horton shushed her. "It's just the placenta," he said. But the nurse was right, and a few minutes later, Connie appeared.

Although both babies were good-sized, they were very different in appearance. Dr. Horton called Jim at work to tell him the news. He could not believe what he was hearing.

After the lengthy hospital stay, which was usual for newborns and their mothers in those days, Mae took Vera and Connie home to Oceanside to meet their sisters and brother.

A Depression-Era Childhood

As Jim Johnson had feared, his masonry business soon succumbed to the dismal economic climate. He then used his business background to run a vegetable market that also sold fish on Fridays. Mae contributed by making delicious pies. She gave them away to customers so they would continue to come and purchase the produce. Finally, Jim became a trucker, spending much time away from home driving back and forth between Long Island and Buffalo. By then the country was beginning to recover from the Depression, but life was still a financial struggle for the family.

One sad day, with tears running down her face, Mae gathered the children around her. "Daddy won't be coming home," she said. "He's gone to heaven." She explained that on one of his trucking runs, their father had suffered a fatal heart attack. The children stayed with neighbors while their mother went with supportive friends to New Jersey for the funeral. He was buried on the twins' sixth birthday.

Nettie, the oldest, had already graduated from Moody Bible College and had married Dave Anderson, another graduate. They pastored in Nebraska and eventually went to Haiti as missionaries. But the rest of the Johnson children were still at home, and at age 46, Mae Johnson had to find a way to support herself and her family.

Sixteen-year-old Mary found a job to help out. Brother Jim, only eight, sold magazines and newspapers and large homemade chocolate mint patties. Mae Johnson worked as a housekeeper, a babysitter, and at a dry-cleaning establishment—anything she could find that would help her keep the family together.

She also cleaned house for a woman in exchange for piano lessons for her little girls. It was not a pleasant experience because, when they made mistakes, the woman would hit their hands with a ruler. When Mae found out, she put a stop to the lessons, and Connie never did learn to play. But Vera's love for piano and classical music grew because a young lady down the street, who was already an accomplished pianist, charged only a small fee to give Vera lessons.

At night, Mae read Bible stories aloud to the children and prayed with them. Vera was greatly influenced by her mother's vital faith, along with that of her sister, Mary.

The family never had much money, but the children felt rich because of their loving relationship with each other and the fun they made together. The Johnsons' series of rented homes were always full of laughter and open to the children's friends. If Sunday visitors dropped in, Mae just added more bread crumbs to the meatloaf or water to the soup.

Mae's faith in the Lord's provision never wavered, even when they had to leave several homes they lived in because the landlords died. On one occasion, their landlord passed away shortly before Christmas. His grief-stricken widow informed them that they had to move out of their home by December 25.

Shocked, Mae said to her, "Do you realize what date that is? It's Christmas!"

"Oh, I'd forgotten," the landlady said. "You can wait until January first to move." That gave them an extra week to find a new home in the middle of New York's cold winter.

Mae went to see a couple who wished to rent out the upstairs of their house. But when they learned she would be bringing four children with her, they reluctantly said, "No. That's too many kids to be living up there."

On Christmas Eve, Mae reassured her family. "Don't worry. God will take care of us." The kids left to carol with young people from church. The carolers' final stop was at the home of a seriously ill woman. After they sang for her, they prayed with her. At the same time, the pastor also prayed that the Lord would provide a home for the Johnson family.

Later that same night, the homeowner who had turned Mae down woke his wife. He told her, "I've been thinking about the

Johnson family. I believe we should let them live in that apartment. What do you think?" The two of them agreed that the family could move in. They called the Johnsons on Christmas morning with the news.

Vera, Connie, and the others rejoiced with their mother at the answer to their prayers.

The Heart of a Missionary

Through good teaching in her church and Sunday school, along with her mother's teaching at home, Vera was well-schooled in the Bible and knew all about the Lord Jesus. But not until she was 11 years old did she realize that she needed to make the choice to follow Jesus for herself.

One evening a visiting evangelist, Percy Crawford of Pinebrook Bible Camp in the Pocono Mountains, brought a quartet of musicians to the church. As Rev. Crawford talked, Vera felt the Holy Spirit drawing her to invite Jesus to live in her heart. She responded, and that night she began a journey with her Lord that would eventually result in a lifetime of missionary service in Alaska.

She continued to grow as a Christian through her church's active youth group and through attending Pinebrook Bible Camp in East Stroudsburg, Pennsylvania, during the summer. She joined a group at her high school called HI-BA (High School Born Againers). They met in students' homes and studied books about the Bible and on finding the will of God. They learned how to be missionaries in their own high schools by carrying their Bibles with them and witnessing to others.

Vera's sisters Nettie and Mary brought many missionaries into their church, and the Johnson family often hosted them in their home. Mary, who was attending the National Bible Institute (NBI) in New York City, became a missionary to Japan in 1951. Vera longed not only to know the Lord better, but also to make him known as her sisters were doing.

While still in high school, Vera worked at a five-and-ten-cent store, earning 25 cents an hour. She later took a job as a switchboard operator with the Long Beach, Long Island, telephone company. Since dial telephones were not yet in use, callers would lift the receiver to reach an operator. The female operator, wearing a headset with earphones and mouthpiece, would ask, "Number, please?" The caller would give her the number, and she would plug corded jacks into a switchboard to connect the caller and the person being called. The work required a good memory, quick hands, and a high degree of accuracy. Vera found much satisfaction in helping her family with the money she earned in this way.

After graduation, she continued the job for a year, earning a living and also saving money for college. She had been accepted at Houghton College in upstate New York. But Mary said, "Why don't you think about attending NBI? It's cheaper than Houghton and closer to home."

Vera visited the Bible institute and realized it would be easier to find a job in New York than at Houghton. "Mary," she said upon her return, "I'll pray about it and check with my supervisor. I'll ask if the phone company will transfer me into New York City. If they'll do that, it will be a sign from the Lord that I should go to National Bible Institute."

The supervisor had discouraging news. "They're changing to dial phones in the city," she said. "They're laying people off instead of hiring them." Even so, the supervisor promised to see what she could do.

Later, she stopped by Vera's work station. "Miss Johnson, I don't know what happened, but we do have a job for you in New York. You can work from six to ten every night. You can keep your seniority, and you'll have vacations off."

Vera's mouth fell open. She knew this was God's sign to her. She would continue to be paid well by the telephone company, so college expenses wouldn't be a problem.

When the next school year began, Vera entered the National

Bible Institute as a first-year student. She enjoyed the classes and opportunities for ministry. She often played piano for services at the Bowery Mission, located at the border between Queens and Manhattan. To reach the mission, she had to take the subway, then walk alone down seedy streets, past homeless men sleeping in doorways. At mealtime, she ate with the men who came to the mission.

She also worked with other students at Momma Short's Mission in Brooklyn, located in the middle of a slum. Part of the students' work was to win entrance to the homes to visit families who lived there.

Al Kelley

In Vera's English class, the students were seated alphabetically. With her last name of Johnson, her seat was next to that of a young man named Al Kelley. He was good-looking, blond, athletic, and 6'2" to Vera's petite 5' 2". A new Christian, he was a little older than the other students because he'd already served in the Army. Before that, he'd boxed and played semi-pro football.

Although he'd been raised in church, he'd heard only a social gospel and thought religion was for children and old women. But after his service in the Army, some neighboring young people from the Priggemier family invited him to go along with them to Harvey Cedars Bible Conference in New Jersey. A man named Jack Murray was preaching, and his wife Eleanor played the piano with fervor. The youth there sang as if they really had something to sing about. Al heard the true message of the gospel for the first time. He pondered it.

Then one Sunday morning, as he walked with his dog in the woods near his home, a Scripture verse he'd heard at the conference came to his thoughts. "Whosoever shall call on the name of the Lord shall be saved." God slammed the truth of those words and the necessity of salvation into his mind and soul. Al fell to his knees right there in the woods. He gave his heart to God, calling on Jesus to save him.

He went home and told his parents that he'd been born into God's family. "Well, that's good," they replied, then added dismissively, "but it will pass."

To their dismay, Al left the family's prestigious church to attend a small, Bible-believing church. There he began to grow spiritually as he worked with young people from High School Born Againers, the same organization Vera had been involved with in high school. He felt a calling to serve the Lord and knew he needed training, but in high school his attention had been directed to sports and he'd not paid much attention to academics. He didn't know if he'd even be accepted into a Bible school.

One day he and the Priggemiers were in New York City for a HI-BA conference. One of these friends was familiar with the nearby National Bible Institute and suggested he talk to the registrar.

The registrar was just leaving when Al walked in, but he took time to talk. He told Al, "You don't have the grades to get in, but because of your newfound faith in the Lord, we'll accept you on probation and see how things go."

So, Al claimed the verse in Philippians 4:13 (KJV), "I can do all things through Christ who strengtheneth me." He entered NBI with a new purpose in life, planning to major in Greek and Hebrew. And that's how he found himself sitting in English class beside pretty, hazel-eyed Vera Johnson, who, it turned out, was also in his Greek and Hebrew classes.

The first morning in English class, the professor asked the students, "What is a gerund?"

Vera answered, "A gerund is a noun ending in 'ing'."

Al, already floundering because he knew nothing about grammar, thought, "I've got to get to know that gal."

After class he struck up a conversation with Vera that ended with her agreeing to coach him in English. She might not have been so quick to agree to the arrangement had she known Al would finish the class with a higher grade than hers. But during the semester, they got to know and like one another. Each felt the Lord was leading them together.

Partners

Both young people joined the North America, Canada, and Alaska Prayer Group that met to pray for the needs of people in those vast areas. It was there they learned about the work of various missions in Alaska.

Vera knew two Moravian missionaries, Mildred Simpke and Loretta Burkhart. The Moravians were known for their work among America's Native peoples. When the women spoke at chapel, Vera's heart was touched. Sometime later, Vincent Joy, the founder of Central Alaskan Missions, which is now called SEND North, spoke to the student body about the needs in Alaska.

Both Vera and Al felt strongly called to go and help. The two were married at the start of their junior year, September 8, 1951, in Vera's home church on Long Island. Because they both desired to present themselves as living sacrifices to God, they took 1 John 3:16 (KJV) as their wedding verse: "Hereby perceive we the love of God, because he laid down his life for us: and we ought to lay down our lives for the brethren."

The new Mr. and Mrs. Kelley had no idea that only five years later, while trying to bring the gospel to a village they had yet to hear of, they would face that verse's challenge for themselves in the frigid waters of Alaska's Prince William Sound.

CHAPTER 2
Into the Wilds of Alaska

The Kelleys' 1952 station wagon bottomed out in another washtub-sized Alaska pothole. Although nine-month old Debbie usually slept in a portable crib behind the seat during car trips, at the moment Vera was cushioning her sleeping daughter in her arms. She tried to absorb the shock with her own body. Debbie whimpered but didn't awaken.

Al gripped the steering wheel and turned to Vera with an encouraging smile. They'd been driving now for 5,000 miles, the last 1,300 over the unpaved Alaska Highway. Knowing that gas stations would sometimes be far apart, they carried extra gasoline. Every night they pitched their tent and camped along the highway, a mosquito net over the baby's crib to keep out the voracious insects. Vera knew she must look as travel weary as her husband. But on this August night in 1954, they would finally sleep in their new home.

Copper Center

In 1937, Vincent and Beckie Joy had begun the work at Copper Center that became Central Alaskan Missions (CAM). Al and Vera would be CAM's newest missionaries. Ever since feeling called as National Bible Institute students to minister to Alaska's Native peoples, she and Al had prayed for the Athabascan Indians of the Interior.

After Al and Vera had married, they finished college together while working with a church in Franklin Lakes, New Jersey. Al took a summer assistant pastorship in an Ohio church between their junior and senior years. By the time they graduated—Al with *cum laude* honors—baby Debbie was on the way. That summer, they worked at a church in Virginia, and in September, the Kelleys celebrated their third wedding anniversary.

Overjoyed when they were accepted as CAM missionaries, they happily visited churches, speaking to people who shared their concern for Alaska. Their baby girl arrived in November 1953. By late summer in 1954, the Kelleys had gathered pledges for the needed support of $300 per month. Bidding farewell to family and friends, they set out on a two-week journey across the continental USA, then northwest through Canada and Alaska. Although they found it difficult to say goodbye, God blessed their travels. They'd had not even one flat tire.

Because another missionary couple from Copper Center, the Parmenters, were on furlough in the Lower 48 states, Al and Vera were asked to fill in during their absence. The Kelleys would live temporarily in the Parmenters' home, the same cabin that the Joys had originally built to live in themselves.

Earlier that day, the Kelleys had stopped at Glennallen, a few miles to the north, where the Joys were then living. Glennallen, the hub of operations for Central Alaskan Missions, lay at the junction of the Richardson and Glenn Highways. Vince Joy's vision of a hospital to serve area residents was coming to fruition in the community. Vince also began a Native Alaskan Bible school, which later became the present-day, fully accredited, four-year Alaska Bible College. Nearby Victory Bible Camp was serving people from all over the state.

The Joys warmly welcomed the Kelleys, and Beckie served them their first moose stew. Vince, a small, dark-haired, energetic man, told them how to find their new home, telling them that some of the women from the church had checked to be sure everything was ready for them. Soon, Vera hoped, they would get to know and love the Alaska Natives they'd come so far to serve.

As they drove along, Al broke into Vera's thoughts. "Did you ever see anything more magnificent than this scenery?"

"No, never," she answered. They both felt awed by the snow-covered Wrangell Mountains looming over the valley. Fireweed massing along the roadside made a brilliant red backdrop for the silky white fluff bursting from its seedpods. The filaments floated past their car windows, announcing that the brief Alaska autumn was on its way. Now and then, they glimpsed the meandering Copper River, pale gray with its load of suspended glacial silt (rock ground to flour by glacier action), and larger than most Alaskan rivers they'd seen thus far.

They passed some cabins scattered alongside the road. Copper-skinned, dark-haired boys and girls played near the cabins. "Oh, look!" Vera cried, delighted. "Indian children!"

The road descended toward the settlement they'd come all those miles to find. Ahead of them, a smaller river, the Klutina, flowed toward the broad Copper. On a bench of land above the road, they spied a 20-by-30-foot building with a steeple, the first church ever built in the area. "It's the Chapel on the Hill!" Al exclaimed. "That's where we'll pastor. Do you remember Vince telling us how soldiers helped him build it back in 1943?"

They turned off the graveled roadway and up an embankment onto the small plateau where the chapel perched. Behind it stood the log cabin that was to be their home for the winter.

A couple of black-haired children stared at the strangers. Al smiled and greeted them. The kids giggled shyly and dashed away. "Maybe they'll be some of our Sunday school kids," he told Vera.

But first, they needed to get settled into their new home. Debbie woke as Vera carried her inside. Al set up her crib, where she played while her parents brought their belongings inside. They were about to begin their year of adjustment to a new climate, a new culture, and a whole new way of life.

Vera and Al were both pleased to discover that the little house had electricity. It was produced by a generator that they would have to ensure kept operating. They also had running water, which was pumped from a well to a barrel inside the cabin.

Although pleasant weather welcomed the Kelley family—summer temperatures in the Alaskan Interior can reach into the 90s—the Joys had told them snow would fly in September, ushering in a long, cold winter with temperatures that could fall into the minus 60s. Fortunately, the Parmenters had left plenty of firewood, and the Kelleys had brought their warm winter clothing from New York.

Making Friends among the Athabascans

More than half the people in the Kelleys' new community were Native or part Native Athabascan Indians. The Native village, where Vera had seen Indian children playing outside their homes, was a little north of the white settlement at Copper Center.[2]

In 1954, most Natives depended on subsistence hunting, fishing, trapping, and gathering of berries (raspberries, cranberries, blueberries, moss berries, and currants). Many still do. The Kelleys admired how they had learned to survive the long, frigid winters and the way they lived off the land. But their hearts broke, especially for the children and young people, at the suffering caused by rampant alcoholism in the community. Al and Vera knew that only the Good News of the gospel could restore the people's self-esteem and set them free from the cycle of alcohol and abuse.

They both worked hard at getting to know the Indian people.

---

2 Copper Center's economy was and continues to be based on local services and businesses. There was a grocery store and a jail. The old roadhouse, Copper Center Lodge, with its restaurant, bar, gas pumps, and rooms for guests, was a center of activity for the community as well as for travelers. In the wee hours of May 20, 2012, the lodge met the fate of so many Alaska history icons when fire—in this case suspected to be electrical in origin—completely destroyed the old building. The National Park Service has offices in Copper Center. (The Wrangell-St. Elias National Park & Preserve is just west of the community.) Tourism is important to the economy. There's also a state-owned 2,500-foot gravel airstrip, not yet built when the Kelleys arrived, for charter flights and general aviation.

Al preached at the chapel on Sundays. They visited in the homes of their Native friends and prayed with them in their struggles against poverty, illness, and addiction. They held Bible studies and taught some of the adults to read.

Along with the Joys and other missionaries, the Kelleys also reached out to people in other communities in the area—Gulkana, Gakona, Chitina, Kenny Lake, and Glennallen—as well as to scattered people who lived away from the towns. Each week, they drove to a home near Kenny Lake to hold a Bible study for local people.

Al joined the men of the community in hunting and fishing. Moose, caribou, and fish became a large part of the Kelleys' diet. Soon after they arrived, Al brought in their first Copper River king salmon, caught in a Native fish wheel.

Vera gasped at the enormous fish. She'd eaten only canned pink salmon before, and didn't care for it. But someone had given her a recipe, which she tried for Al's fish: Spread a brown paper bag on a cookie sheet. Gut a fresh, whole salmon and place it on the bag. Slide it into an oven and bake for one hour. Remove from the oven, peel off the skin, and eat. Prepared in this way, Vera discovered that the salmon was moist and tasty. They found later that local people also ate the crispy skin.

Although early Russian Orthodox priests had never entered the Copper River Valley, the Ahtna tribe of Athabaskan Indians, who traveled widely in their fishing, hunting, and trading with other Native groups, learned about the Orthodox religion and set up their own Russian Orthodox church in a log building in Copper Center. Since no priest directed the services, lay readers called the people together and read from the liturgy.

Vince Joy had often visited one of these lay readers, Jim McKinley, who could read only at a second- or third-grade level. Because of Jim's alcoholism, he didn't want to hear what Vince had to say. Sometimes he threatened to throw him out of the house. But Vince persisted in telling him the gospel message, until one day Jim broke down, confessed his sin, and accepted Christ as Savior.

The next time Jim rang the bell to call people to the Russian Orthodox church, he stood before them and said, "You need to go to the Chapel on the Hill because they teach you the Jesus way. I was your leader, but I was just reading words to you. I didn't even understand what I was reading. But now I know that Jesus is the only Way."

That was a turning point for the Natives in Copper Center. While the Kelleys remained there, people continued to come to know the Lord. The Kelleys helped several gain victory over alcohol as they began their walk with the Lord, stood beside them in their struggles, and even taught some of them to read so they could see for themselves what the Bible had to say.

Four Native men from the area, including Jim McKinley, eventually became pastors. Harry Johns was from Copper Center as well, and Ben Neeley and Fred Ewan were from Gulkana. They'd all been alcoholics with very little education because like many of the Ahtna children, they'd traveled from camp to camp with their parents, fishing and hunting. As a result, like Jim, they achieved no more than a second- or third-grade education. But when these four men preached, God used them. Their messages were simple but from the heart, and they led others to know the Lord.

Eventually all four men completed three years of Bible-school training and met other requirements for ordination. In 1972, at the close of that year's Native Bible Conference, they were ordained by Glennallen Community Chapel, by then a fully independent and self-governing church. Jim became the pastor of the Copper Center Native Church.

The winter of 1954–1955 sped by for the Kelleys, with their busy ministry at the Chapel on the Hill and in the surrounding settlements. Besides the regular services, they also organized activities for the young people and get-togethers for the women. Vera played piano in the chapel but took her accordion when they visited surrounding villages. Little Debbie attended these meetings in her pajamas. As days went by, Al and Vera proudly watched their daughter learn to walk and talk.

A highlight of this time came in April at the Easter sunrise service. Though the weather was still cold, 100 bundled-up people gathered on a hill overlooking the frozen Copper River. By six a.m. the sun lit up the Wrangell Mountains and sparkled off the snow while people sang triumphant songs of Easter. Vera's heart swelled with joy at the Lord's blessings. Brown faces and white reflected her smile as she held Debbie close and listened to her husband retell the glad story of Jesus's love for all. This was why they'd come to Alaska. No matter what the future held, she knew it was worth it all.

A New Direction

Over the winter, Vincent Joy discussed with the Kelleys the need for a Christian witness in the village of Tatitlek, which from Valdez was 30 miles across Prince William Sound. The isolated community was populated mostly by Alutiiq Eskimo people whom the locals called Aleut. They had a different culture and language from the Athabascan Indians in Copper River Valley. Vincent hoped the Kelleys would take the gospel to that strongly Russian Orthodox village.

After a year in Copper Center, Al and Vincent drove the 100 miles to Valdez. This little town on Prince William Sound was where many men had come in the late 1890s, searching for an easier route to the Klondike gold fields. At first, prospectors made the grueling trek over Valdez Glacier and down the Copper River to Copper Center. Some stayed to search for gold, while others went on to Dawson City in Canada's Yukon region. Soon, the US Army sent explorers to rediscover an old Indian trading trail that led from Prince William Sound, up through the Keystone Canyon, and over Thompson Pass. Eventually, that trail became the Richardson Highway between Valdez and Fairbanks in Alaska's Interior.

The town of Valdez had been built on gravelly outwash from the Valdez glacier.[3] When Al and Vincent arrived in Valdez, they hired someone with a boat to take them across the Sound to Tatitlek. Vincent had often spoken of his burden to reach out to isolated settlements around Prince William Sound. Al and Vera felt excited to think God might use them to reach an area that had no gospel witness. But to live there, they'd first have to obtain permission from the villagers.

As the boat drew near to the little settlement sheltered at the foot of Copper Mountain, Al noticed the Russian Orthodox church's blue, onion-shaped dome. He knew that Alutiiq people had historically been heavily influenced by Russians, who'd claimed the area before Seward's purchase of Alaska in 1867. But he also knew that no permanent priest lived in the village, nor was there a doctor. Perhaps the 80 or so people there would welcome missionaries.

Stepping onto the dock to greet the solemn-faced men who came to meet them, the missionaries asked to see the village chief. To him they stated the reason for their visit.

The chief was polite, but not enthusiastic about their request. "The council will have to meet and discuss what we will do," he said.

"How soon do you think that will be?" Vincent asked.

The man shrugged. "Can't say. Some of them are gone, fishing."

It was late in the day, and the wind had come up on the Sound. Vincent and Al decided to spend the night on the boat and return ashore in the morning. Later that night, Al woke and looked out at the village. Rippling above Copper Mountain were swaying curtains of blue-and-green light . . . the aurora borealis.

---

3   This proved to be an ill-chosen location, for in the powerful Good Friday earthquake of 1964, those deposits collapsed into the Sound, taking with them the dock and about thirty people on the dock, and sent a huge wave inland that destroyed boats, buildings, and oil storage tanks. Afterward the townspeople moved the town to a safer spot four miles away.

Their glow illuminated the tiny settlement at its base, as if God were giving a sign that he was claiming the village for himself. Undoubtedly the Enemy would fight, Al mused. But with God on their side, they could do anything. Al couldn't wait to get started.

CHAPTER 3
Shipwreck!

New Challenges

After the village council met to discuss Al and Vera's desire to come to Tatitlek, it sent word that the Kelleys were not welcome to live in the village itself. The missionaries were disappointed but not discouraged. They had already identified an alternative place where they could live. The site of the Ellamar copper mine lay only half an hour's walk from Tatitlek or 15 minutes by skiff. A cannery had also operated there. Both the mine and the cannery were closed, but the buildings remained, along with a caretaker and a few Native families. The Kelleys got permission from the cannery owner to live in Ellamar's abandoned schoolhouse.

Vincent Joy, along with Vincent's father, accompanied Al, Vera, Debbie, and their spaniel Chubby to Valdez, where they again hired a fishing boat for the trip across Prince William Sound. From the dock at Ellamar, they hauled their belongings to the schoolhouse, then carried them upstairs to the building's second floor. They had purchased a package of hamburger in Valdez to fix for dinner, but discovered that Chubby had found it first and eaten it.

Al turned to set an armload of boxes down. "Ouch!" he exclaimed. He'd bumped his head on the ceiling, only the first of many times it would happen. The roof formed such steeply slanting walls for their living space that he could stand erect only in the center of the floor. "It's okay," he told Vera. "When we get the downstairs fixed up for Sunday school and meetings, I'll have plenty of space to stand up straight."

After committing the Kelleys and their new ministry to the Lord, Vincent and his dad returned to the mission at Glennallen. The Kelleys' first order of business was to find some sort of boat in order to carry on their work in Tatitlek. They purchased and repaired an open, 20-foot skiff of the sort used by fishermen there and bought a newly-overhauled 25-horsepower outboard motor.

Al and Vera began by using the skiff to motor the 15 minutes from Ellamar to Tatitlek, and even made several trips back and forth across the open water to Valdez before winter winds made that impossible. Al realized they had much to learn in the way of seamanship and discretion in handling such a craft on the Sound's treacherous waters. Weather there was much different from the extreme low temperatures and dryness of interior Alaska. This was a damp, penetrating cold accompanied by the north wind's continual howling. When they went somewhere in the skiff, Al would cover Vera and Debbie with a tarpaulin to shield them from the wind. They asked their supporters to pray for a larger, enclosed boat that would allow them to carry God's Word throughout the entire area surrounding Prince William Sound.

They were glad to get repairs made in the house and a large, wood-burning "drum" stove installed downstairs before winter set in. They knew that snowfall in the region was among the heaviest in the world, sometimes completely covering houses. And sure enough, that winter, a total of almost 15 feet of snow fell.

Beginning a Ministry

As they got acquainted with people, the Kelleys found many of them to be open and friendly, although alcohol was as big a problem in Tatitlek as in many other Alaskan communities. Al and Vera visited in homes with their little girl. The schoolteacher at Tatitlek allowed them to hold a Bible study in his house. It wasn't long before his wife, Beverly Scoggins, and their 12-year-old son

David put their trust in the Lord. Al wrote that young David's testimony impressed people in the village. After experiencing a hunting accident in which he was shot through the neck, he told people that he was not afraid to die because he was ready to meet the Lord. This impressed the Natives because their ritualistic religion left them no hope or assurance of heaven. Fortunately, David did recover.

The Kelleys learned to live like the people in the village. Although they had no electricity, they joked that they did have running water. They had to do the running for it! They carried it from the stream behind the house and poured it into a 50-gallon drum for storage. Al used a wooden yoke over his neck and two five-gallon cans to carry the water. Debbie would go with him to the stream, riding on one of the cans. Eventually, the family acquired a small propane refrigerator to keep food cold in the summertime.

For protein, they ate mostly bear meat. That area had no moose, but in addition to the bear, there were also some deer, seals, fish, and plenty of clams. Along the shore in front of the house, they dug their own shellfish, including some huge razor clams and geoducks. They found small ones, too, called steamers. Vera wrote home, asking, "How do you cook clams?" Her mother, being from Long Island, New York, knew lots of ways to fix them. She sent Vera a collection of recipes.

The mail plane came once a week; the mail boat, once a month. The mail's arrival always caused celebration. The Kelleys might receive several sacks full at one time, and of course, they especially enjoyed letters from home. The mail boat also brought their grocery orders, mostly canned goods and nonperishables. They had to plan ahead for months in advance.

Some village people began visiting them in Ellamar. Al and Vera invited parents to send their children to Sunday school classes in their home and used the skiff to bring them over. All the children of families living at Ellamar came, as well as some from Tatitlek.

Vera wrote, "The gospel was very, very new to them, and it was a real thrill to see the Holy Spirit begin to work in their hearts. Five young boys and two girls from Ellamar, as well as three older girls from Tatitlek, have made decisions for Christ and really seem to mean business. Pray much for these young Christians as their attempts to live for Christ are met by opposition and discouragement in their homes."

As happened in other villages, Tatitlek's Russian Orthodox Church had no regular priest, only a lay reader. Unfortunately, he drank right along with the other commercial fishermen who spent most of their salaries on alcohol.

Opposition

Meanwhile, because of drinking and fighting caused by the use of alcohol in Tatitlek, some people moved over to Ellamar. They not only came to Sunday school themselves, but they also brought children from Tatitlek along. Then, about a year after the Kelleys moved to Ellamar, the presiding Orthodox bishop came to Tatitlek for his yearly visit. When he learned that some of his people were attending the mission Sunday school and church, he was furious. He told the people, "If you continue to go there, you will be excommunicated from the Russian Orthodox Church."

That church was all the people had known throughout their lives. At that time and place, Russian Orthodoxy used fear and superstition for control. As a result, many people stopped coming to the mission services, and after the bishop's visit, the Kelleys carried on with a greatly reduced Sunday school. They realized that they were in a spiritual battle for the souls of people, but that nothing was too hard for God. The villagers remained friendly and allowed them to visit and distribute literature.

The village chief kept watch on those who went to Ellamar on Sundays and listed their names to send to the bishop. Then the chief's wife passed away after a heart attack brought on by heavy drinking. The Kelleys grieved over the hopelessness that accompanied death in the village. The people had only the often-repeated ritual to go over again and again in a vain attempt to reach the throne of God. A priest from another village, Chenega, came to hold the funeral, during which he read aloud another letter from the bishop, absolutely forbidding the few who had ignored his first ultimatum to attend the missionaries' services.

After fishing season ended, the bishop came to baptize new babies and do weddings. Then he called the people on the chief's list up in front of everybody and made a public example of them. That made folks even more fearful to associate with the Kelleys, although some continued to come to Sunday school.

One of the villagers, Virginia Paulson, was only eight or nine years old at the time. Vera had the delight of leading her to the Lord. More than 50 years later, Vera visited her in Anchorage. Even though Virginia's life had not been easy and many family members were affected by alcoholism, she'd remained faithful to God. She'd married a godly man, and both she and her husband loved the Lord.

One day Virginia looked at Vera and said, "You seemed to be so happy when you were in Ellamar. Even though you were far away from your family and your home and you didn't have running water or electricity, yet you were happy."

Vera simply replied, "Well, we knew we were where the Lord had sent us."

A New Baby

In May 1956, the Kelleys traveled to Glennallen to await the birth of their second baby. Al occupied the waiting time by helping to build a house for Dr. Pinneo, the new doctor. At that time, the medical facilities consisted of just a two-room shack. When Vera went into labor, she was put in one of the rooms. Al had gone to town with Dr. Pinneo, but got back just in time.

Dr. Schneider was in the other room attending the woman who owned the I Bar F Bar. Someone had kicked a stool out from under her, causing her to fall and break her leg. The nurse got Dr. Schneider's attention just in time for him to deliver 11-pound Tommy. Vera was amazed at the ease of the delivery—and at the baby's size. He was a beautiful baby, happy and content.

The Kelleys returned to Ellamar for a busy summer and fall, although opposition to their ministry continued.

If enough children lived in the village, the government provided a teacher. But when one of the village mothers contracted tuberculosis and she had to go to a hospital in Seattle for treatment, all of her seven children were taken out of the village, leaving too few children for a school that year. The families who had moved to Ellamar wondered if classes could be held in the schoolhouse. They asked Al and Vera if they would teach school that year, using a program provided by the government. They agreed and sent for the teaching materials, but their plans to become schoolteachers were interrupted.

An Ill-fated Trip

Central Alaskan Missions personnel met monthly at Glennallen, but with winter fast approaching, the Kelleys knew they would probably be isolated at Ellamar for months. They wanted to attend one more CAM meeting—the one in November—if possible. By then they had a larger boat, christened the *Evangel*, to use in getting back and forth to Valdez.

When they left the morning of November 7, they planned to retrieve their car at Valdez and then drive the 100 miles to Glennallen. As mentioned in the Prologue, fifteen-year-old Jim Paulson, Virginia's older brother, was excited to be with the Kelley family on this trip into the Interior. He had never been away from Tatitlek. He'd never seen moose or even a rabbit.

After the *Evangel's* engine quit and Al left, rowing the eight-foot skiff into the churning waves and whirling snowflakes to get help, the storm increased. Vera gave the baby his bottle and fixed peanut butter sandwiches for Debbie, Jim, and herself, but her queasy stomach made it impossible for her to eat. *Al must have made it home by now. Surely, help will come soon.*

Darkness came early. Huge swells continued to pound the *Evangel*, and still no help arrived. Jim took a look around the boat, then, with a glance at wide-eyed Debbie, he whispered to Vera, "We're starting to take on water, and I think we're closer to the shore now than we were."

"God will take care of us," she reassured him. But when she put the children to bed on the bunk, she left them dressed in their warm clothing and snowsuits. She lay down beside them but couldn't sleep. *Where, oh where, was Al?*

Early the next morning, she heard Jim on the deck, pumping water out of the boat. The wind was still howling, and the boat still tossed. Suddenly Vera felt the boat rise up, up, up on a huge swell. Then came a jarring crash. Was Jim okay?

She heard Jim shout, "Jump!" and she thought help had come. But when she scrambled on deck with the children, she saw Jim out on the rocks along the shore. She handed Debbie down to him, then quickly wrapped the baby in an army blanket and handed him to Jim as well. She had time only to grab a sleeping bag and jump onto the rocks herself before the *Evangel* was washed back into the water.

She could think only of the next big wave sweeping them into the Sound along with the boat. Fortunately the formation where they stood had ledges stair-stepping down to the beach. Peering through thick-falling snow, she helped Jim get the children off the rocks to the sand and then up into the thick forest.

They knew they had to find shelter from the wind and sub-freezing temperatures. The soggy forest floor felt spongy underfoot. Thick foliage dripped cold water and snow on them. As they moved deeper into the woods, the wind was less cutting, but everything that wasn't frozen was wet. Jim stopped to look around, then led them toward a protected spot beneath two crisscrossed fallen trees. The short winter daylight would soon be completely gone.

They had no food, no water, not even any matches to start a fire. Al had been carrying the container of waterproof matches in his pocket when he left.

Debbie clung to her mother's leg and whimpered. The baby, who seldom cried unless he was hungry, decided he was hungry and wailed. They were all shivering from the cold. With shaking hands, Vera unzipped the double mummy sleeping bag she still carried, pulled out the insulated liner, and gave it to Jim. They crawled beneath the shelter of the fallen trees and wriggled into the sleeping bags. Vera took the two little ones in with her to try to keep them warm. Later, Jim took Tommy into his sleeping bag and Vera laid Debbie on her own stomach to keep her warm.

For Vera, the long, inky black night was sleepless. Jim Paulson snored softly beside her, as peacefully as if he experienced such adventures every night. The children squirmed and cried out in their sleep. Vera's feet, clad in galoshes over her saddle shoes, ached with cold. Still, she prayed, "Jesus, thank you for being with us."

Trees creaked and groaned in the wind. Waves crashed over the rocks on the shore. Blobs of snow dropped from the trees, and branches cracked now and then. Were they in danger from trees falling on them? Or from wild animals? "Protect us, Lord."

How would searchers even know they were here, hidden deep in the forest? "Father, please watch over Al."

Exhausted, she finally fell into a fitful sleep. She woke when Tommy wailed. Jim handed him over and crawled out of his bag. Gray light filtered through the branches overhead as he disappeared toward the beach. The baby needed a diaper change, but Vera had no diapers. And he was hungry. He'd sprouted his first teeth early, and she'd weaned him over a month ago. She tried to nurse him but had no milk to give.

She eased herself out of her own bag, leaving Debbie asleep with the baby beside her, and tucked Jim's insulated liner over them as well. Then she made her way to the beach. The wind still blew, and a mixture of rain and snow slanted down. No boats broke the expanse of tossing gray water. She saw Jim rounding a point.

He shouted something, beckoning to her to come. She scrambled toward him. Had help arrived? He shouted again, and this time she caught his words. "I found the boat!"

The *Evangel* lay washed up in a cove not far away. As they approached, Vera could see that the boat was in shambles. They climbed aboard to search for food, but the food locker had been smashed. They found a can of bear meat that Vera had put up, along with mustard, ketchup, and a soggy piece of brown bread. The rest of the food had washed away. They did find many cans of motor oil, useless for their needs, and a wet mattress, which they dragged back to their shelter. They also found their suitcases, with the contents completely waterlogged.

"Maybe if we put some of these wet clothes along the beach, searchers might see them and know we're here," Vera suggested. But even as she said it, she knew no one would notice something that small in the vast expanse of rugged shoreline that must be searched.

They huddled in their shelter all that day, through the second night, and through the third day, waiting for the storm to break. Vera tried to melt snow in her bare hands to keep the children hydrated. They sucked on icicles. Throughout the third night, Tommy fussed continually. His cries grew weaker. Heartsick that she could do nothing for his hunger, Vera held him against her chest inside the sleeping bag and crooned to him. At least he was warm. Finally, he grew quiet. Vera thanked the Lord that he'd fallen asleep, and she dozed off, too.

When she woke in the morning, Tommy lay very still in her arms. His face was pale and cold. Alarmed, Vera shook him. "Wake up, Tommy. Wake up."

But she couldn't waken him. Her little boy had died in the night.

CHAPTER 4
A New Ministry

Sad Rescue

As Vera gazed down at the still face of her little son, her heart broke. Knowing that if she gave in to the tears threatening to gush forth, her body would lose hard-to-replace water, she held them back. Instead, she bowed her head over Tommy's small form. "God, thank you for loaning us this precious child for the past six months. I give him back to you. I know you'll take good care of him."

Beside her, Debbie whimpered. Teenage Jim made his way through the trees from where he'd been scanning the churning surface of Prince William Sound. He shook his head. "No one's coming yet," he said.

Then he caught sight of Vera's face. By his expression, she knew he'd guessed what had happened. Mutely, she handed Tommy to Jim and squirmed out of the sleeping bag. Together, they wrapped the baby's body in the army blanket and laid it in a sheltered spot a little distance from their makeshift camp. Then Vera returned to her daughter.

Another day and night passed. Finally, the roar of the wind lessened. The waves quieted. Sometime the next morning they heard a motor, but by the time they reached the shore, it had passed. They saw an open skiff in the distance, heading away from them toward Valdez.

"It's the schoolteacher's boat," Jim said.

They found out later that when the teacher reached Valdez, he noticed the Kelleys' boat, the *Evangel*, was not moored at the dock as it should have been. He found a telephone and called the mission headquarters at Glennallen. No, the Kelleys hadn't arrived for the meeting.

The alarm went out. Small planes and a helicopter crisscrossed the Sound. Boats from the villages joined them, scanning the shoreline for signs of life. Vera and Jim could hear the activity and even see the planes, but they weren't close enough to signal the searchers.

Another night passed. As Sunday morning dawned, they saw a boat coming their way. Jim ran to the water's edge, shouting. Vera sounded a fog horn they'd salvaged from the *Evangel*'s wreckage. The noise got the boaters' attention. They saw the little group on the beach and pulled to shore.

Vera's thoughts jumbled in relief and sorrow. How could she tell Al that Tommy hadn't survived? But as the rescuers jumped from the boat, she saw that Al was not among them. And in the confusion of greetings and explanations, she gradually understood that they thought Al was with her. That meant he had never reached the village.

Someone went back into the woods with Jim to get the baby's body.

Then the rescuers helped the castaways into the boat and gave them dried fish to eat. The warmth of the cabin felt heavenly, but Vera soon became aware of a terrible burning in her feet. Someone helped her take off the rubber galoshes she'd been wearing since she left Tatitlek. The rubber had been slit and torn by sharp rocks along the shore. Though she hadn't realized it then, water had seeped in. Her feet were frozen.

Back in Tatitlek, rescuers took her and Debbie to the schoolteacher's house. Village friends came by to see them. Although Debbie had lost a lot of weight and a rash covered her body, she was fine. Other than a frostbitten heel, Jim was okay too. But Vera's feet swelled, and she knew that without treatment, gangrene could set in.

The villagers tenderly cared for Tommy's body, but didn't let Vera see it. The women fashioned flowers to adorn a tiny casket, made by the same chief who had sent the names of those attending the Kelleys' services to the bishop. He carefully lined the casket with cloth.

While the search continued for Al, a chartered plane flew Vera and Debbie to Valdez, where they spent the night at the hospital. The next day, Dr. Schneider came to drive them to Faith Hospital in Glennallen. Dr. and Mrs. Pinneo cared for Debbie during Vera's hospitalization.

Many searchers looked for Al—on foot, with dogs, and using an Army tugboat. Eight months later, they found pieces of Al's skiff on an island about four miles from Ellamar, but they never recovered his body.

Comforted

Grieving in her hospital bed, Vera felt God's peace and grace as he wrapped her in his love. She found comfort in reading her Bible. One of her favorite assurances was Psalm 18:30 (KJV): "As for God, his way is perfect: the word of the Lord is tried: he is a buckler to all those that trust in him." Strength also came from the hymns of the church and the prayers of God's people.

While in the hospital, Vera received an encouraging letter from author Elisabeth Elliot, who had grown up near Haddenfield, New Jersey, where Al was raised. Elisabeth's missionary husband, Jim Elliot, had been one of the five missionaries slain by Huaorani warriors (known at that time as Auca Indians) in Ecuador during an attempt to bring them the gospel in January 1956. The Kelleys' accident happened the following November. To Vera, it seemed that her missionary work in Tatitlek had come to a dead end, but Elisabeth wrote, "There are no dead ends in the life of God's child." Though Tommy and Al were now with the Lord, Vera was reminded that God had spared Vera's life, and Debbie's, for a purpose. In the deep waters of personal tragedy, she felt the Lord God to be closer than ever.

The loss of Vera's loved ones had softened the hearts of the Natives at Tatitlek and Ellamar. She felt they were ready for the gospel. Many people assumed that because Vera had always seemed so dependent on Al, she would not stay in Alaska without him. But Vera said, "God didn't call just Al. He called me, too."

Return to Alaska

When Vera's feet had healed enough to allow travel, she and Debbie returned to New York for an emergency furlough. In spite of her sorrow, Vera was grateful for the time with loved ones. She even got to see her sister Mary, a missionary to Japan, after almost six years apart.

While in New York, Vera told her story at Shelton College, from which she and Al had both graduated. She told the students of the need for workers in Alaska. In response to her testimony, several of them dedicated themselves to mission work. One couple came to join Central Alaskan Missions.

Once her feet greatly improved, Vera and her little girl returned to Alaska. That June, Vera sailed to Tatitlek with missionaries Joe and Peggy Virgin and stayed to help them get started. Back in Ellamar, the sight of her weather-beaten schoolhouse-home revived overwhelming memories. She bowed her head, realizing her own insufficiency and utter dependence upon the Lord, and prayed for special strength for the task that lay ahead.

Joe Virgin had to repair the skiff that was their only transportation outside of foot travel. Walking back and forth to Tatitlek with Debbie and the Virgins' baby boy took them an hour each way.

Peggy was a nurse, and the people appreciated her medical services. The missionaries received many promises that the children could attend Sunday school, and on the last Sunday in June, 19 children from Tatitlek showed up. But by September, the many who had been faithful in attending the services had again been forbidden by the bishop to come and were threatened with excommunication.

This opposition from the Russian Orthodox Church made it too hard for the Virgins to stay. Another couple, the Hubers, tried to work there too, but their church withdrew support because they couldn't show tangible results. When no missionary was able to continue the work, Vera wondered how people in Tatitlek would come to know the Lord, but God had other plans. At separate times, he sent Christian schoolteachers, the Autens and the Meekers, to live in the village and show God's love to the people. The villagers remained close to Vera's heart.[4]

A New Beginning

Then, at the seeming dead end to Vera's ministry, a new beginning opened up for her. While she was at Glennallen, the headquarters for Central Alaskan Missions, Vincent Joy asked her if she would stay on as the mission bookkeeper.

Thus began a new and unexpected ministry; one which shaped and prepared Vera for a job God had in mind for her far in the future, in a distant place called Kako.

So Vera moved with Debbie to Glennallen, which was still a very small mission. Vince Joy was doing much of the work himself, including building the new Faith Hospital, which would eventually employ a number of nurses and two doctors. The radio station and Bible college were still in the dreaming stage.

At first the bookwork followed a simple plan, with the missionaries doing their own receipting. But when Vera took over the bookkeeping, they called in an accountant who helped her set up the books for Central Alaskan Missions. She learned and grew, along with the mission.

---

4   God was faithful to grow the seed Al and Vera had planted. Today Tatitlek has a sound Bible-believing church, which is pastored by a Native couple.

Her days were full, but going to bed at night without Al beside her was incredibly lonely. She read many of Elisabeth Elliot's books, among others, and found them encouraging. Somewhere in Vera's reading, an author compared life to being like either a mirror or a window. If she approached life as a mirror, she'd see only herself, with her pain and misfortunes. If she simply waited for people to reach out to her to meet her needs, she would end up throwing a pity-party as the only one in attendance.

Sometimes she lay in bed at night, crying out and sharing her sorrow with the Lord. Then he'd help her get her eyes off herself and onto him and his Word. He promised to bring her through her grief, and she would look through the "window," seeing other people and their hurts. "My opportunity to reach out and minister to them," Vera said later, "was God's cure for my loneliness."

She leaned on the promise in 2 Corinthians 1:3–4: "The God of all comfort . . . comforts us in all our troubles, so that we can comfort those in any trouble with the comfort we ourselves receive from God."

"It's a chain reaction," Vera later reported. "God put his arm around me to comfort me; then I put my arm around others who were hurting and shared his comfort with them."

Being the mission bookkeeper worked well for Vera. She could do the work at home and still take care of Debbie. If people dropped by to talk, she could make up her hours at night. She also taught in the Native Bible school, which at first was primarily for the villages of Copper Center and Gulkana. She showed women how to use flannel-graph lessons and hold Sunday school for the children. Teaching English classes and Bible studies was a joy, as was working with young people in teen clubs.

The mission started an outreach to the village of Mendeltna, 35 miles from Glennallen. On Sunday, Vera would drive there with some of the nurses to help. She took her accordion, and later a little pump organ, which she played for the Sunday school that was held in the home of an Athabascan couple, Joe and Morrie Secondchief.

Morrie had come to Mendeltna from Cantwell. In the late summer, Morrie and other village women invited Vera to pick berries with them. Like everyone who harvests berries in the Alaska bush, they knew to keep watch for bears that might be grazing in the same berry patch.

Morrie told Vera about the time she'd taken her teenage grandchildren along as bear guards on one of her blueberry picking expeditions. After a while they got bored and told Morrie, "Grandma, be your own bear guard." They wandered off, leaving Morrie with their .22 short-barreled gun. It was loaded with one .22 Short (half-size) bullet, generally useful only for small game, such as squirrels and rabbits.

After Morrie had picked a while longer, she heard crashing in the brush. A bear rushed directly toward her with its mouth wide open. She had time only to raise the gun, jam it into the bear's mouth, and pull the trigger. She let go of the gun and scrambled away, not looking back. Later she sent the grandkids to look for the gun and also for the berries she'd been picking. They found the bear lying dead. Incredibly, the bullet had angled through its body and gone straight to its heart.

Vera's brother, Jim Johnson, a carpenter, had been deeply touched when Jim Elliot and the other missionaries had died in Ecuador. When Al Kelley disappeared, his brother-in-law wrote to find out if Central Alaskan Missions could use his skills. The mission welcomed the offer and accepted the Johnsons in June 1959. Jim, his wife, Vi, and their three children left Florida on October 15 and arrived in Alaska on October 28. Winter was well underway. They lived in a trailer home beside Vera's residence through the minus-30-degree weather. Jim helped build the log chapel at Mendeltna, which Vera attended, and he also built some of the mission buildings at Glennallen, including the log home the Johnsons lived in, the nurses' quarters, and other structures.[5]

5   The Johnsons worked with CAM for many years. After retiring and settling at Mendeltna, they continued to minister on their own for another

Vera found that her cure for loneliness lay in reaching out to others. She needed adult fellowship, and Debbie needed to be around other children, so Vera frequently invited families in for meals. She continued to do the bookkeeping at home. The mission grew, with the hospital providing care for Native and non-Native people alike.

Vincent Joy's dream of a radio station was realized when KCAM went on the air in March 1964. The station carried the gospel into the bush where missionaries couldn't go. People heard the Word and were saved through the radio programming. Christian music was also broadcast, and four times a day, the *Caribou Clatter* program sent messages to people in the bush who had no telephone access. A storekeeper could post a message notifying a customer that his grocery order was arriving on such-and-such a plane. Hospital patients could let their family members know when they were coming home.

The Bible school expanded its focus from training Native pastors and workers to becoming Alaska Bible College and offering a four-year degree to students from all around the state.

The mission named its new administration building after Al Kelley and put his portrait on display, along with a brief summary of his life and death. After the building was completed, Vera moved into an office there and kept regular business hours. Each day, Debbie called the office when she arrived home from school so her mom would know all was well.

In August 1966, CAM's founder passed away after a brief illness, and Joe Virgin became the acting general director in Vincent Joy's place.

In 1971, Central Alaskan Missions merged with Far Eastern Gospel Crusade. Since that name was inadequate to cover Alaska, in 1983 it was changed to SEND International. Leander Rempel became the director of SEND North, headquartered in Glennallen.

---

10 years before moving to Anchorage to be closer to medical treatment for Jim.

Also in 1971, Vera was due for another furlough, but Debbie wouldn't graduate from high school for another year. Then she planned to go to Biola University (then Biola College) in Southern California for nurse's training. Vera postponed her furlough until after Debbie's graduation so the two of them could travel to New York. Debbie took a year off before starting college. They made the circuit of various churches that supported the work of SEND North, updating them on the work and needs of the mission. Then they drove back to Glennallen, following the route that Vera had traveled with Al and Debbie when the family had first gone to Alaska.

The Big City

During that furlough year, Vera heard from Director Rempel. "Would you consider going to Fairbanks?" he asked. "The white churches are not really reaching out to the Native people there. We've been requested to start a Native church. I've asked the Gerdeses to go there, and we need a single person to join them. You seem to be the happiest when you are teaching the Bible. You have the gift of teaching and could complement the team in Fairbanks."

Vera's first reaction was, "No way! I don't want to go to a city."

She'd found her comfort zone in little Glennallen, which had a population of only a few hundred. She loved her log cabin home, and having her brother Jim nearby was special as well. Although she knew a few people in Fairbanks, she'd be starting over in an urban environment. Although Alaska's second-largest city would be considered only a town in most places, Fairbanks had traffic, stores to supply every need, and it also hosted the respected University of Alaska. It was the transportation hub and supply center for the state's vast Interior region. Living and working there would be a huge change.

Vera prayed long and hard about what she should do. She remembered the promise in Isaiah 58 that said when we are obedient to the Lord, our lives are like well-watered gardens. Above all, she wanted God's will in her life.

One night while speaking at a church, Vera showed slides of the needs in Alaska and asked people if they would be willing to go and help. At that moment she felt God pointing his finger at her. "You're asking them, and you're not willing to go to Fairbanks?" She felt convicted and told Leander Rempel she would accept the assignment.

Soon after Vera and Debbie returned to Glennallen, Debbie left for college. Although Vera had prayed much for the Lord's will concerning a move to "the big city," it wasn't until she made a visit to Fairbanks and returned to Glennallen that she felt a deep sense of peace that "this is the way, walk ye in it."

On October 23, 1973, as she traveled the 250 miles up the Richardson Highway to her new life in Fairbanks, Vera found again, in the uprooting and starting over, that God drew her closer to himself. And the years ahead would prove to be some of the greatest of her life.

CHAPTER 5
Fairbanks: Alaska's Largest Native Village

Getting Started

Ben and Daisy Gerdes, the other members of the team, had already settled in Fairbanks. Vera found an apartment and began attending Denali Bible Chapel, a nondenominational group that was sympathetic to the needs of Native people. Soon she became part of an extended family of friends and like-minded people.

The team's first task was to locate Native people who had come from many villages in hopes of jobs, education, and the advantages of city living. Unfortunately, many became overwhelmed by the change. Fairbanks offered the same temptations that had dragged them down in the villages. Vera wondered where they were living. How could the team get to know them?

The intent was to eventually start an indigenous Native church. From the beginning, the team prayed for God to bring a Native leader for the work.

Vera went with the Gerdeses or other partners to low-income housing areas to make initial contacts. She'd knock on a door, introduce herself, and after visiting a while, ask, "Are you attending a church? If not, are you interested in coming to a Bible study?" Some people *were* interested. So the team invited them to come to their homes for Bible study. Soon there were two Bible studies: one for women, and one for men. Alcohol was an ever-present problem for the Natives, but God worked in hearts, and lives began to change.

That Easter, Vera traveled south to Tok to join the people

THE STORY OF DAVE AND VERA PENZ

from Tok Chapel for an outdoor sunrise service. She played piano accompaniment for a choral group singing an Easter cantata, and then, as they worshiped on a snow-covered hill surrounded by majestic mountains, they heard wolves in the distance as if joining in their glad refrain. Back in the chapel, Vera gave a Scene-O-Felt lesson, *The Resurrection Miracle.*

On Sunday afternoons, she helped the Gerdeses begin a combination Sunday school and church service at Denali Chapel for Native people. Many Natives who were students at the University of Alaska attended. Occasionally, Native gospel teams from other areas would come and bless them with their ministry. Wycliffe missionaries Dave and Kay Henry also helped. The team began a Friday night Native fellowship with Christian films, Native speakers, and potluck dinners.

At the end of her first year in Fairbanks, Vera rejoiced that many doors, once closed to them, had opened. She'd spent hours visiting people—making new contacts as well as strengthening former relationships. She tried to be available when people needed help. She provided transportation to and from the hospital, the detox center, and the rescue mission. She visited hospitalized people and those in a care center. She ran errands and opened her home to listen, encourage, and pray for those who needed help and victory over alcohol.

Still, she realized a great need remained for a Native pastor to work with the indigenous people.

Expanding the Outreach

In her September 1975 letter to supporters, Vera exclaimed that summer temperatures had reached a high of 93 degrees, a welcome contrast to the long, cold winter months. Also, her work was not limited to the urban scene in Fairbanks. While headquartered there, she had opportunity to travel throughout much of the state. Starting in May of that year, she'd flown into Tanana, a village populated with both Athabascan Indians and whites, to speak to women at a Mother's Day banquet. She also got to stand on the bank at the junction of the Tanana and Yukon rivers, watching the ice break into huge chunks that went grinding and jostling past, on their way to the sea.

The village of Eagle, Alaska, across the Yukon River near Dawson City, Yukon Territory, became one of her favorite places to visit. That summer she helped fellow missionaries hold a "trail camp" for a group of 6th-, 7th-, and 8th-grade girls from Eagle. On the riverbank outside the nearby village of Chicken, they set up tents made from plastic sheeting, slept with mosquito netting over their heads, cooked their meals over a campfire, hiked, and swam in Mosquito Fork River. Vera taught the girls games from her own youth and led them in their Bible-study time each morning. One young lady thanked Vera "for being young again."

In August, Vera and Debbie flew to Nome, their first visit to an Eskimo town, where Vera was interviewed by the local Christian radio station about the mission's work, and she gave her testimony at a Sunday evening worship service. She and Debbie also took a side trip to the village of Teller to see a herd of reindeer.

That December, in stark contrast to summer's warmth, Fairbanks temperatures spent more than a week at minus 50 to 60 degrees, with ice fog dropping visibility to 75 feet. Since conditions were too hazardous for driving, thus canceling most activities, Vera spent the time baking Christmas cookies for ladies in the Native Bible study.

Then she had the fun of traveling to California, where her daughter was studying, and spending Christmas with Debbie.

Ministry through Hospitality

A large part of Vera's ministry focused on opening her heart and home to others. In a letter summarizing the work for 1976, she quoted Isaiah 58:10–11 (NASB), the passage that had helped her discern God's direction regarding her move to Fairbanks. "If you give yourself to the hungry and satisfy the desire of the afflicted, then your light will rise in darkness and your gloom will become like midday. . . . You will be like a watered garden, and like a spring of water whose waters do not fail."

Then she listed some of the people who'd enjoyed the hospitality of her home that year. One woman from Eagle, for whom Vera had requested prayer in the past, came with her son, planning to divorce her husband. She stayed three weeks, spending much time talking and praying. God changed her heart and attitude, and she returned to her husband. Her husband also trusted Christ, and they set out to rebuild their marriage.

For two weeks, she hosted four young summer missionaries. Then her Native friend Elizabeth Pete came from Copper Center for a week. They visited Native homes together, and Elizabeth shared her testimony in Bible studies, at the rescue mission, and at local churches. Vera said, "Oh, for more Elizabeth Petes here in Fairbanks!"

Other visitors were women who needed time away from home to view their problems from a different perspective; missionary wives in town to shop, share their burdens, and pray; and people needing a home away from home while tending to medical needs.

Also, Vera's 86-year-old mother, Mae Johnson, made her seventh trip to Alaska to see her daughter in Fairbanks and her son and his family in Glennallen. The time with her mother brought Vera great joy. Vera said, "She made many lasting friends. Those who met her loved her."

Debbie spent the first four summers with her mother. Each summer between her school years, she was offered employment at the Fairbanks hospital: first as a pediatric nurse's aide, next on the medical and psychiatric floor, then the surgical floor, and lastly, again in psychiatrics. She loved it all, and the experience was invaluable as she began her nursing career.

After graduation, Debbie married Mark Holland, a young doctor in training, and she became a nurse at a Sacramento, California, hospital.

Encouragement

Elisabeth Elliot—the author whose writings were of great encouragement to Vera after her husband and little son died—wrote a book called *Twelve Baskets of Crumbs*. In it she said, "Nothing is meaningless. Nothing, for the Christian, is a dead end. All endings are beginnings." Reading this, Vera thought back over her life and was reminded how God had met her in each ending, and how each time he gave her a new beginning. Her move to Fairbanks in 1973 had been one such time.

She found great happiness in her ministry as people came to know the Lord and some were freed from the curse of alcoholism. Native Fellowship nights continued on first Fridays, with the intent of reaching whole families. The team continued to pray that more men would be interested.

Further Equipped for the Work

By 1979, Vera was on furlough again, traveling in her 1978 Dodge Aspen from meeting to meeting, telling about the mission work. She also attended a three-week seminar on alcoholism and drug abuse. Out of the 44 professionals involved, she was the only missionary. She then took a course on biblical counseling.

Since an important part of Vera's ministry was to reach out to Native women who were struggling with alcohol, both courses were of great help in her ministry. That fall, when she spoke at the annual Village Advance at Victory Bible Camp, she shared principles she learned during her courses concerning the chemically dependent and their families. Then she gleaned feedback as she and her fellow missionaries compared notes on how to deal with the problem of alcoholism.

An incident from those years in Fairbanks tells of the kind of work she sometimes found herself involved in. Vera calls it her "bar-hopping story."

Dwayne King, a pilot friend, needed to find an Athabascan woman, Adeline Potts, who'd grown up on the Yukon River and later married a white man. Dwayne enlisted Vera's help in finding Adeline, an alcoholic who drank even more than her husband. Vera and Dwayne went to the many First Avenue bars, looking for her. In the first one, someone recognized Vera and exclaimed, "Mrs. Kelley, what are you doing *here?*"

She explained, and he told her, "Adeline's in the next bar over." She and Dwayne found Adeline and persuaded her to leave. They sobered her up and talked to her. She and her husband both became Christians through the love of believers in Fairbanks. They attended Bible school, and later, after the Iron Curtain fell in the 1980s, spent some time in Mongolia as missionaries.

Eagle

After Vera returned from furlough, among the many speaking engagements she had that fall and winter was one in Dawson City, where she shared some of the concepts she'd brought back from the seminar on alcoholism. Since there was room in the plane, she'd invited Ruth Sauer, a friend from Denali Bible Chapel, to go along. Ruth and her husband were responsible for getting Focus on the Family films by Dr. James Dobson into Alaska, and she had a deep interest in Vera's mission and also in Dawson City.

When they left Dawson City, the pilot decided to go through customs at tiny Eagle, on the Alaska side of the Yukon River, rather than at the larger Fairbanks International Airport. Vera was delighted because she knew many people at Eagle.

After clearing customs, the pilot suggested they visit a family Vera also knew. The parents had just adopted four nieces and nephews whose mother and father had recently died in a plane crash. This expanded their family to eight children, some of them teenagers. The wife had been struggling with the whole situation and had been praying she could talk to Vera. And here she was! While they all joined in prayer for mother and family, the oldest daughter hopped on her snow machine and rounded up several more ladies who were hungry for encouragement and fellowship.

Ruth was touched by the scene and arranged to send the Dobson films for people in Eagle to watch.

Vera returned to Eagle before Christmas to spend time in Bible studies and to visit Native and white villagers' homes. God was at work in the lives of her friends there. Another woman from Eagle came to Fairbanks for medical reasons. Her medical report was delayed, so she spent the weekend with Vera, and on Sunday evening, Vera had the joy of pointing her to Christ. She went home to fellowship with the believers in Eagle.

Living the Life

As the decade of the '80s began, Vera was carrying on the work alone, since Ben and Daisy Gerdes had gone on to work elsewhere. Vera asked her supporters to pray for the right couple to further the work, and God sent a missionary couple, working in Tanacross, to help twice a month with the Friday Native Fellowship. The Lord also sent Lynne Hounsell, a single woman who'd been working with the summer missionary program for eight years. As Lynne assisted Vera with her work, they became good friends.

In May 1980, word came that her older sister, Mary Johnson, whose faith had so greatly encouraged Vera as she grew up, had died suddenly. Mary had served the Japanese people in their homeland for 29 years. One night, on her way home from teaching a Bible class, she was hit by an 18-year-old driver who was drunk and high on drugs. Mary died four hours later.

Three days later, on a plane to Japan, Vera sat beside a young man who had recently attempted suicide. He asked if meaning and fulfillment could be found in going to church. Vera told him that he could find these things in a person, Jesus Christ, and shared with him the prayer of faith. She trusted that he later prayed it and in so doing would become the first person to accept Christ as a result of Mary's untimely death. She also tried, without success, to talk to the young man who had been responsible for the accident. She asked her supporters to pray that he would trust Christ.

Progress

By now the monthly Native Fellowship had 30 to 40 members and continued to grow. She hoped a Native church would emerge from this group, one of her goals in coming to Fairbanks.

On Good Friday evening, a Native lady read aloud, in her own language, a recently completed translation of the crucifixion and resurrection Scriptures. Another woman told how it touched her to hear the story in her heart language. "It's like I heard it for the first time!" she said. Wycliffe translators Dave and Kay Henry were the ones who'd made it possible.

Vera's ministry to the people of Eagle continued, both when people came to Fairbanks for varying reasons and when she flew to the village to visit and lead Bible studies. On one occasion, she flew to Eagle to attend the funeral of a young man who had taken his own life. As her plane landed, she saw another plane taxiing down the main street toward the airstrip. Also coming down the street were a truck, a snow machine, a man with his dog team, and a horse pulling a sleigh. "Where but in Alaska!" she exclaimed. Then her thoughts turned to the people she worked with. Their needs were as diverse as the methods of transportation she'd just witnessed, and God cared for them all.

Evidence of God's provision was a new couple, Wayne and Doris Eames, who had joined the Fairbanks team. Also, Native men were participating in the Friday Night Fellowship meetings— an answer to prayer.

On March 5, 1984, Vera's 93-year-old mother, Mae Johnson, passed away after a fall. At the service, Vera and her siblings were together for the first time since Vera's wedding in 1951. Afterward, her sister Nettie and husband Dave Anderson came to spend the summer hosting the Chapel on the Hill at Copper Center. Now a historical site for tourists, this was the chapel where Vera and Al ministered their first year in Alaska. That summer, Dave Anderson spoke at the Native Bible Conference held in July at Copper Center, and a group from the Friday Night Fellowship attended.

At the end of August that year, Vera left for Long Island and a year's furlough, following which she drove cross-country to Marysville, Washington, to see Debbie, Mark, and the two little grandchildren. Back in Fairbanks and moving into a different apartment, she was encouraged to see new faces at the Native Fellowship, and best of all, the male leadership they'd been praying for.

Fritz and Yvonne Geffe, graduates of Alaska Bible College, joined the Fairbanks team when their support was complete. That team included Wayne and Doris Eames, Lynne Hounsell, and Vera, all from SEND North. Also included were George and Judy Richardson and Violet Warman from Inc. (AMI), and Dave and Kay Henry with Wycliffe, on loan to AMI. These people met weekly to pray for one another and their Native friends.

The Native Church Begins

In March 1986, Vera announced the beginnings of the Fairbanks Native Bible Church. They met each Sunday evening in homes. Native men were taking leadership and sharing the Word. She was thankful for Fritz Geffe's involvement and his fresh insights from Scripture. By summer, the Native Sunday school and church service were meeting on Sunday afternoons at Denali Bible Chapel. The next step would be to have their own meeting place.

Vera quoted what her husband Al Kelley had written in September 1954 during their first year at Copper Center: "It is a challenge to try to prepare these Christians here to reach their own people. Their testimonies and changed lives will be of infinite help to us as we go to start a new work."

He had been writing concerning their upcoming ministry in Tatitlek, but in her March 1986 newsletter, Vera pointed out that his words came to pass 30 years later in Fairbanks, when believers from Copper Center and Gulkana arrived to share the gospel with Native people there.

Adventures in Ministry

That summer, the mission purchased a duplex. After lots of painting of walls, ceiling, and woodwork, Vera moved in to the lower unit. She had a garage (much appreciated when temperatures hit 30 below zero or colder) and a large backyard. The unit's three bedrooms made her ministry of hospitality much easier. In one week she had guests from Eagle, Glennallen, Pennsylvania, and New York. The Geffes moved into the unit above hers.

Vera continued to counsel and encourage people, leading some to new life in Christ and others to draw closer to the Lord. She was saddened by those who rejected the teaching of God's Word while choosing to return to their old lifestyle. But she was not discouraged. "The future is as bright as the promises of God," she said.

In October 1986, Vera was thrilled to return to Tatitlek and visit people she'd ministered to many years before and who had been transformed by the good news of Jesus Christ.

She spent Thanksgiving with a family—Cindy, Bob, and three-year-old Tara—who lived above the Arctic Circle at Chandalar Lake and were the only residents there. Vera and her friend and fellow worker Lynne Hounsell flew in with the Boones, missionaries in Bettles, who went to see the family twice a month for Bible study and fellowship. Vera brought a turkey and other goodies for the holiday feast. While there, the temperature dropped to minus 55 degrees. One night, frantically barking dogs alerted them to a prowling, hungry grizzly bear that should have been hibernating. Bob fired shots into the air, hoping to scare him away. When the sky lightened the next day, they saw its big tracks. It had smelled the bait for Bob's traps inside the garage and had slashed the door open searching for it.

The next night, Bob slept with his clothes on, and Vera kept a gun under her bed. At 2:30 a.m., the dogs howled again. Vera woke Bob. He went out and found that the grizzly had killed two of the tethered dogs. He ran back inside. Cindy was sleeping soundly, so he told Vera he needed help to bring his other dogs back to the cabin. Vera threw on her winter gear and grabbed a second gun and a searchlight. They found two other dogs dead as well. They brought the one survivor back to the cabin and then saw the grizzly in the shadows burying the dogs. Later, the bear moved into the light. Bob stepped just outside the door and fired one shot. The bear spun and ran off.

At that time of night, they decided not to try to learn if the bear was dead or only wounded. In the morning Bob found its body lying beside the garage. His one bullet had passed through the lungs and heart.

Back in Fairbanks, believers in the Native Bible Church continued to share their faith with others. In February 1987, a group of 10 drove 100 miles by bus to participate in the Native Musicale in Anchorage. That event had begun in the mid-1960s when a small Christian boarding school, Victory High School (a partner of Victory Bible Camp), encouraged students to share their Christian testimonies and music, as well as their culture, in a program they called the Native Musicale. In 1974, the Anchorage Native New Life Fellowship took over responsibility for the event.

Also in 1987, a gospel team of six young people flew with Native Fritz Geffe to the Eskimo villages of Tuntutuliak, Bethel, and Eek to share God's love through testimonies, skits, and music. And at the Fairbanks Rescue Mission, several Native Church members shared testimonies and song.

Fritz Geffe became the pastor of Fairbanks Native Bible Church. Eventually the congregation built a beautiful log building on the Chena River. The prayers of many years had been answered!

And so the Fairbanks years went by, 15 of them, years of stretching and growing. Vera enjoyed her busy ministry. Life was good, and she felt content.

Then came a phone call that changed the direction of her life once more.

Barge at Kako Landing on the Yukon River, showing caterpillar road to KRC
Credit: Gordon Bakke

Sandra Kozevnikoff in Hooley Lodge with photo of Ed and Joyce
Hooley. Ed was her school teacher in Russian Mission many years prior.
Credit: Joan Husby

David Penz, 1955
Credit: Jeanne Rodkey

Penz family near Anchorage, mid-70s: Diane, Jan, Dave, Valerie, Jeanne, and Jonathan
Credit: Jeanne Rodkey

CHAPTER 6
Dave's Story: A Life of Hard Work

A Missionary's Beginnings

Born in 1934, David Carlton Penz might have felt right at home in Garrison Keillor's fictional Lake Woebegone. Dave's parents, dairy farmers in southern Minnesota, lived about 10 miles from Rochester, the closest city. They were strict German Methodists, at church every time the doors opened.

Dave's father, Carlton Penz, taught Sunday school and served on the church board. As a young man, Carlton had hoped to be a missionary and attended Bible school for a year. Then his own father fell from a ladder, injuring his back. The older man wrote to Carlton: "You must come home and run the farm or I'll have to sell it."

Carlton prayed for direction. The answer came as a strong feeling that he should return home to manage the farm. If he did, he felt God's assurance that he would have sufficient income to support other missionaries. As a young teen, Dave saw God's promise fulfilled when his father was able to fully support a missionary couple in Honduras for two years. Not only that, when the couple returned from their period of service, Carlton gave them a new car.

The family often entertained missionaries in their home, and Dave greatly admired these servants of God. As early as the first grade, he knew the Lord had something special for him to do.

One day in his small country school, the teacher asked the

three first-graders what they wanted to be when they grew up. Little Betty said, "I want to be a farmer's wife."

Dave didn't say he wanted to be a preacher, because he knew all the other kids would tease him. He didn't want to lie and say he wanted to farm. So he merely sat with a grin on his face and said nothing. The teacher said to Dave, "Maybe you'll think of something," and went on to the next child.

By the time she came back to Dave, he had thought of an answer that still kept his secret. "I want to be what my uncle is."

At that time, his mother's seventeen-year-old brother was helping in the church's youth group. This young man was good to Dave and took him fishing, and of course Dave loved his uncle. Eventually the uncle left to attend university. When he came home for a visit, he took Dave—barely big enough to see over the dashboard—for a ride in his car. Dave never forgot the conversation that ensued.

"You know the Bible we read?" his uncle asked. "It's all fairy tales. Don't believe any of it."

Crushed and disillusioned, Dave thought, *I can't trust anything he says anymore.*

Farm Boy

Dave, the eldest, had four brothers and a sister. As soon as the Penz youngsters were big enough, they helped with the farm work. Dave's parents expected him to set an example in industry and character for the others.

When Dave was about four years old, he was supposed to watch his one-and-a-half-year-old brother while his parents milked the cows before breakfast. They told him to keep the child out of the seed corn, which was piled on the porch in white sacks, ready to sell to farmers for planting. But little brother wanted to climb on the sacks, which got them dirty.

Over and over, Dave pulled the toddler down. He didn't have the maturity to find a distraction for his brother. Finally, he got so frustrated at the child's disobedience that he took it out on himself. He went to the window and pounded on the glass until it broke. The glass cut his finger tips. When his mother came back to the house, she found him bleeding profusely. He carried the scars throughout his life.

By the time he was 11 or 12, Dave was doing a man's work on the farm tractor. When neighbor kids asked, "Can you play?" he'd say, "I've gotta work." His brothers would run off to play, and Dave would do their work too because he was the oldest and his dad had put him in charge. But he resented being asked to do more than he was able.

What Dave didn't realize at the time was that with no mufflers installed on the tractor, the resulting loud noise was damaging his hearing.

In addition to helping with farm chores, Dave kept a flock of chickens as soon as he became old enough to care for them. Every night after school, he collected and washed eggs and placed them in cartons. He sold them for 20 cents a dozen to earn spending money.

Hard Times at School

Dave's early school years were difficult. Not only did he have heavy responsibilities at home, but school was also hard for him. The one-room building was crowded with at least 30 children of all ages being taught by an overworked teacher.

Dave was unable to begin first grade on opening day because he was sick with measles. When he finally showed up several weeks late, all the chairs were taken, so the teacher temporarily sat him on a little table beside her desk.

He looked out at all the eyes staring back at him. The kids teased, "Teacher's pet! Teacher's pet!" Feeling miserable, he ran home at recess. His dad found him crying under bushes behind the house. Assuming that Dave simply didn't want to go to school, he spanked him and sent him back.

Most of the school children came from Roman Catholic homes; the Penz home was Protestant. At the time, the two divisions of Christianity had little understanding or acceptance between them, and the Catholic children picked on Dave because he was different. For the first few years, some of the boys would line up to block the road leading off school property. They wouldn't let Dave cross the road to go home, but would jump him and take him down.

When America entered World War II in 1941, many teachers joined the military or went to work in factories that produced equipment for the war effort. In the Penzes' farming area, there was such a shortage of qualified teachers, they had to hire whoever would take the job. For the next four years, Dave and the other children learned very little at school.

One day after Dave had started fifth grade, his mother asked him to read some 4-H club papers for her. Shocked to find her son couldn't read, she told her husband. His dad was so angry, he called a meeting of the school board members, none of whom still had children in school. Carlton Penz agitated for a new school board and good teachers. He searched for a teacher and found an 18-year-old Christian girl who'd had a year of teacher's training. After she was hired, Carlton told her, "If you have any trouble with the kids, let me know."

Although he supervised the installation of bathrooms with chemical toilets to replace the outhouses, he wasn't able to arrange for a new well at the school. They still had to haul in drinking water, but at least the children had better learning conditions.

The teacher roomed and boarded at the Penz home for the next two years and tutored Dave after hours. He did learn to read, though not fluently. But she helped him so much that he passed state boards with the other two students in his class and graduated from the eighth grade.

God's Leading in the Early Years

When Dave was 10 years old, a missionary from Nigeria was

scheduled to speak at church. The Penzes invited the man to have dinner with them before the service and then spend the night. That evening, after the missionary had presented his message, Dave asked him questions about his work.

The missionary said, "Dave, I want to talk to you about something." The two of them went out the backdoor and stood in the dark for a few minutes. The missionary put his hand on Dave's shoulder and said, "I feel that God has his hand on you, that he wants you to be a missionary." Dave listened and pondered, but he didn't tell anyone what the man said because he didn't yet know the Lord for himself.

Later, while in bed one night, Dave confided to his brother that he thought God wanted him to do something special for him.

"Not me," said his brother. "I just want more pigs, more cows, a bigger farm."

"But what's going to be most important when you stand in front of Jesus?"

"Don't talk to me about that stuff, Dave," his brother retorted, "or I'll kick you out of bed!"

During that time in Dave's life, one of his jobs on the family farm was feeding the pigs. One big sow was about to have her first brood of piglets. As the time grew near, the six-foot-long, 900-pound animal became jittery and unpredictable. Then something set her off on a rampage.

She crashed through the walls of the pigpen and ended up in the horse barn inside a 20-foot pen. Dave managed to close the gate on her and left her there to have her litter. She promptly killed the newborns. Even then she didn't settle down, so Dave's father decided to leave her there. He told his son to put her food in a big pan and slide it between the rails of the fence. At chore time, Dave did as his father suggested, but the sow, snorting with anger, grabbed the pan and flung it across the pen.

Dave couldn't reach the pan to retrieve it, so he waited until the animal appeared to be sleeping. Just in case she awoke, he put some food in a bucket to distract her and quietly climbed the fence into the pen. Before he could reach the empty pan, the beast was on him, mouth wide, fangs bared, screaming in rage. He held the bucket between them, hoping she'd take the food, but she grabbed it, bit down hard, and flipped both the bucket and Dave through the air to the back of the pen. She was on him in an instant, savagely snapping at his neck.

Dave flung his arms up. "God, help." And he felt God tell him what to do.

Dave stiffened two fingers and thrust them up the sow's flaring nostrils. She backed away, shook her head, then roared after Dave again. But by now Dave's dog had jumped the fence and was chewing at her flanks. The pig whirled to fight the dog while Dave scrambled to safety.

The close call convinced him, young as he was, that the missionary was right. God had something special in mind for Dave. At the age of 13, he put his trust in Jesus as his Lord and Savior. For two or three summers after that, his father let him leave farm work long enough to attend the Evangelical Church Bible camp. Each year Dave took further steps in his growth as a Christian.

One summer on the last night of camp, the speaker placed a book with blank pages, like a guestbook, in the front corner of the room. He asked, "How many of you this week know God is talking to you about your lives? Does anyone feel God wants you to be a preacher? Do you feel God might want you to be a missionary?"

Several kids walked to the front and wrote down in the book what they felt God was telling them. But Dave was so shy, he sat squirming in his seat. He knew God wanted him to respond, but he was too scared to walk up the aisle. Finally, the leader said, "Maybe you don't feel you could preach, but you could do something with your hands, and you feel God wants you to do that."

I could do that, Dave thought. He walked to the front and wrote in the book, "I could help someone plant potatoes."

Would he really plant potatoes for the Lord? All he knew was that God wanted him to do something for him, and in the doing, Dave would use his hands.

For high school, Dave went to Rochester Consolidated School. He hated academic classes because he couldn't read fast enough to keep up. So he took what he considered to be "easy" classes: agriculture, wood shop, and welding. He had learned to weld before he reached ninth grade. When he enrolled in the welding class, the teacher told him, "You're so good, you can teach the other kids." So the teacher worked on his own John Deere tractor in the shop while Dave taught the students how to weld.

Although he found reading difficult, Dave did read one particular book in the ninth grade that deeply impressed him. *A Man Called Peter* by Catherine Marshall told the story of Catherine's husband, Peter Marshall, a godly Scottish immigrant who became the US Senate chaplain from January 1947 until he died in January 1949.

In the preface, Catherine told of a dream she had after her husband's death. Peter was working among the roses in a heavenly garden. He told her he knew she was writing a book and said: "It's all right, Kate. Go ahead and write it. Tell it all, if it will prove to people that a man can love the Lord and not be a sissy."

Marshall's beautifully written, masterful sermons and prayers touched Dave's heart. He cried as he made his way through the book, and God used it to work in his life.

One evening when Dave was in 10th grade, he sat in the church balcony with other kids and watched a missionary film called *Wings Over the World*, put out by Jungle Aviation and Radio Service (JAARS), the aviation and radio arm of Wycliffe Bible Translators.

In the film, two young men headed into a South American jungle to work with a tribal group. They walked the jungle trails for an entire week to get to a little village, where they built a shack and began learning the language. They were there only a short time when one of the young men came down with appendicitis. They had no way to get help, and it was too far to reach a doctor. He died, and while his friend and the villagers dug a grave near the cabin, an airplane flew across the mountain and out of sight. The missionary stood there weeping. "God," he said, "if we'd had an airplane, this wouldn't have happened."

The missionary went home, learned to fly, and started a missionary aviation organization.

Dave felt strongly that God wanted him to become a missionary and also to learn to fly. When he told his girlfriend, Carmen, about his desire, she said, "I don't think I want to be a poor missionary's wife," and broke up with him. Dave was heartbroken for awhile but soon began looking for another young woman, one who would understand his call to ministry.

Love at First Sight

Although Dave was in the tenth grade, he was still doing seventh- and eighth-grade work under the tutelage of his teacher, who boarded at their house. Her younger brother rode over every weekend with their father to pick her up and take her home. This brother now and then invited Dave to come spend the weekend with him. Then the two boys would go over to a cousin's family and play with the eight boys there.

One day, the boys' sister came out of the house, all dressed up and ready to go to town with her dad. Dave's eyes bugged out. *Cute as a button*, he thought. Love at first sight! Dave was seventeen, and Janet Mulholland was only 14 or 15. But he felt positive she was the one for him.

Love at First Flight

Meanwhile, Dave couldn't get his mind off learning to fly. When his flock of chickens grew to 500, he began to save his egg money. When he had $10, he went to the airport after school and paid for a flying lesson. After his first time in the air, he was hooked.

Now, not only did he need to pay for lessons, but he also wanted to buy his own airplane. Two years later, when he turned 19 in 1954, he'd saved up $600, equivalent in today's money to about $8,000. That was enough to buy a used Piper J-3 Cub and learn to fly it.

He'd do his farm chores, then go flying. But about six months later, Dave received his summons from Uncle Sam to serve in the Army.

His brother asked to buy the plane, but every time he got in to take a lesson, he'd get airsick. So Dave parked the plane in a farm shed and off he went to Fort Leonard Wood, Missouri, for basic training.

In the Army and Close to Death

According to Army custom, Dave and his company were assigned to a cadre of professional servicemen who trained the new unit. Unfortunately, some of these men were far too fond of liquor, and they took their aggression out on the new recruits to the extent of preventing them from sleeping at night. They'd roust the young men out of bed to spend hours cleaning the barracks or to make them clean and reclean their rifles. Dave had no time at all to think about being a missionary, or even to read his Bible.

The trainees became sleep-deprived and worn down. After six weeks, Dave contracted pneumonia. Along with five or six others, he went to sick call. But the doctor didn't even examine them. He barked, "You guys are just trying to get out of work. Get out of here, or I'll send you to jail." Since the doctor refused to listen, Dave went back to work. He got weaker and weaker and finally passed out.

His comrades carried him to the hospital. He had a collapsed lung, pneumonia, and bronchiectasis.[6] He couldn't get enough air into his lungs and went into a coma. The Army sent word to his

6   Bronchiectasis is a localized, irreversible dilation of part of the bronchial passageways caused by destruction of the muscle and elastic tissue.

family, "Your boy's not making it. You'd better come if you want to see him alive." His mother and dad did come for a day. Although Dave was unconscious most of the time, he was aware of his mom's fervent prayers for him.

Later, while Dave still lay unconscious, he felt a presence on the bed beside him, near his right hand. A voice spoke to his spirit, "Dave, you quit playing games with me, and I'll let you live."

He responded, "Okay, Lord, I'll be serious with you." He opened his eyes, but no one was there.

A medic saw his head move and came running. He said, "What can I do to help you, soldier?"

Somewhat confused, Dave asked, "What did you do with the things in my shirt?"

Happy that Dave was alert enough to talk, the medic showed him his belongings in the stand by his bed.

The hospital was a barracks building over 100 feet long, with beds spaced two feet apart. During his first week there, four other men died of pneumonia. All the doctors could do back then was to give penicillin, morning, noon, and night. Dave later said, "They shot my butt till I looked like a pincushion."

He began to get better. Though he'd been in the hospital for three months, the doctors still hadn't diagnosed the problem with his lungs. Finally, they gave him a two-week pass and sent him home.

At home, he relapsed and became very sick with a high fever. His father took him to see a doctor friend who was associated with the Mayo Clinic. The doctor told the elder Penz, "I've got a new, powerful antibiotic the Army doesn't even know about. I'm going to try it on your boy."

The doctor tried the new medication. Right away, Dave felt alive again. But the doctor said, "You're still too sick to go back to work. I'm going to request another two-week leave of absence for you."

He sent word via the Red Cross to Dave's commander that

he would be late in coming back to Fort Leonard Wood. After a month at home, Dave took a bus back to the base. On the bus, he met a man he knew, Bud Enstrom, a chaplain's assistant from the University of Minnesota. He was staying in a building near Dave's barracks.

When Dave tried to check in with his unit, he was told he'd been AWOL. "If you show up around here," the sergeant yelled, "I'll call the MPs to haul you away."

Not knowing what else to do, Dave got up every morning for roll call. Every day the sergeant cussed him out and chased him away. When Bud Enstrom learned of Dave's trouble, he suggested, "I think we should tell the chaplain about your problem."

When the chaplain investigated, he found Dave's paperwork from the Red Cross lying untouched on the wrong person's desk. The chaplain arranged for it to be sent on to the proper person. When Dave showed up for roll call the next day, the man who'd been screaming and cussing him out said, "There's been a bad mistake here. Bring your stuff, soldier. We're going to put you in a different outfit."

Dave still had a year to go in the service. The Army sent him to a different school, in Lawton, Oklahoma, where he learned about electronics and military radio communications.

After graduation, he and 5,000 others got their orders to ship out for Korea. In the town of Everett, Washington, Dave made his last calls to Janet—who by now was his fiancée—and to his family in Minnesota. He boarded the troop ship in the evening, where he was assigned a bunk in the front hold next to a bulkhead. He and the others were so tightly packed in their vessel, they felt like canned sardines. The ship steamed out of port in the dark, through the Strait of Juan de Fuca, and headed north.

CHAPTER 7
Detour to the Future

On the open ocean a day later, the ship encountered a fierce storm. Soon, many of the 5,000 men were feeling queasy, then seasick. They lined the railings, "feeding the fish," as the wind increased and the ship wallowed in 100-foot waves.

Everyone was told to get inside, close all the doors, and stay in their bunks. These narrow beds were stacked five high, and when occupied, sagged like hammocks. There was so little space between them that when a man turned on his side, he bumped the man lying above him. The hold was a chaotic place, with seasick men groaning, throwing up, and holding onto their bunks to keep from being tossed to the floor. The stench was horrible.

Dave was one of the few who didn't get sick. When someone was needed to run a movie projector in the dayroom, he volunteered. The dayroom's location, near the center of the ship, minimized the pitching and wallowing. Still, he watched the movies mostly by himself. Everyone else was too sick to come. He stayed there for the duration of the two-day storm.

The soldiers hadn't been told that the ship would be stopping at Alaska's port of Whittier, an Army facility hurriedly built at the onset of World War II, for some of their number to be redeployed.

Reassigned

When the ship steamed into harbor, Dave's name was called over the ship's loudspeakers, along with those of the other men in the forward hold. That's how he was informed of his reassignment to become a radio operator in Alaska. Because it was too dark and windy to dock, the ship anchored in the bay all night.

At daylight, the ship nudged into the dock. Snow covered nearby low buildings as smoke puffed up through their buried stovepipes. A train waited beside the dock. Two huge buildings loomed incongruously at the base of Maynard Mountain. Although he later learned that the mountain was in the Chugach Range, he scarcely noticed it now—or the large buildings at its base. One of the buildings housed the soldiers stationed at Whittier and was later made into condominiums that sheltered nearly all the communities' inhabitants. The second multi-storied building held businesses needed to support the Army installation and the community. That building was nicknamed "The City Under One Roof."

All of the 72 soldiers whose names had been called had received communications training. They'd been chosen to serve in Alaska, where the new Nike missile defense system had just been installed. However, because it wasn't yet operational due to unexpected difficulties, the redeployed soldiers were needed to staff the old Arctic anti-aircraft guns until problems with the missiles could be solved. Dave and the others grabbed their gear and boarded the train. Soon they were chugging through three and a half miles of tunnel before they emerged on the other side of the mountain range. The train then followed a long fjord, called Turnagain Arm, to Anchorage.

At nearby Fort Richardson, Dave didn't get his new assignment right away because it took the Army a while to decide where they wanted him. The fort had a fancy barbershop, but the barber had been rotated out of the Army. The new men were asked if anyone could cut hair. Never afraid to try something new, Dave thought it couldn't be too hard to give an army haircut. So he volunteered.

Perhaps it was the awkward way Dave picked up the clippers, but his first customer eyed him with apprehension. "How much experience have you had?" he asked.

"Oh, I've cut lots of hair," Dave assured him, thinking back to his time on the farm. He remembered how he'd shaved around the udders and bellies of the milk cows so the manure wouldn't stick to their hair. "I trimmed the hair off the bellies of 30 milk cows every three weeks."

The horrified customer, still wearing the cloth around his neck, headed for the door.

Dave learned to give a military haircut and remained a barber for two months, until he received his assignment as a radio-telephone operator for a 120-mm-gun outfit. Those anti-aircraft guns could shoot five miles high and seven miles out. Each gun occupied a six-foot-high revetment dug into the ground, and each of four revetments, placed about 100 feet from the others, formed the corner of a square. The idea was to box any enemy aircraft flying overhead in the center of the four guns, which would then fire simultaneously. Dave worked in one of these revetments next to a radar unit. He was responsible for the radio and phones and keeping in touch with all the other outfits every two hours.

As part of his job, he had to teach some of the other men how to climb telephone poles, using a belt and spurs. The trick was to lean back against the belt so the spurs would dig into the wood. But some newbies found it hard to trust the belt. Instead, they'd lean in to grab the pole with arms and legs. Their spurs couldn't dig in at that angle.

One day an overconfident soldier named Creech got partway up the pole on his first climb, looked down, and panicked. When he grabbed for the pole, he started to slide. The pole by then was so covered with splinters from other mens' spurs, it looked like a porcupine.

As Creech slid, the splinters stabbed the inside of his legs and crotch. Though the onlookers shouted for him to lean back, he was screeching so loudly he didn't hear them. He spent a miserable afternoon at the hospital having the splinters removed, wishing he'd trusted his safety belt.

Finding Fellowship

Dave's shift was eight hours a day, just like a regular job outside the military. The first time he earned a pass to leave the base, he caught a bus to Anchorage's Fourth Avenue. As he got off and the bus pulled away, he stood on the curb, praying. "Lord, I don't know a church or anyplace where I can find other Christians."

He looked toward the east and saw a sign that said, "The Church of the Open Door." Having known a good church by that name in Denver, Colorado, he walked up the street to the little log building. Finding the door unlocked, he went in and found a room full of soldiers sitting with open Bibles. They gave him a friendly greeting and an invitation to join them. Dave found they were studying a Navigators[7] lesson and memorizing Scripture verses.

Dave learned that military men were welcome to hang out at the church. There was even a room in back where they could sleep and eat. He met the pastor, John Gillespie, who later became the director of Arctic Missions Inc., now known as InterAct Ministries. Dave loved the preacher's expository Bible teaching, and soon he felt at home in the Church of the Open Door.

Meanwhile, since he knew he'd be working at Fort Richardson for the next year, he called his fiancée, Janet, and asked if she would come to Alaska. "We can get married here," he suggested.

Eighteen-year-old Jan agreed to come. When Dave's two brothers traveled the Alaska Highway to Anchorage for a visit, Janet rode along. When they left, she stayed behind and took a door-to-door job selling china dishes. She also worked at a day care. Vivacious and beautiful, Jan loved talking to people. She did well at both her jobs, saving all the money she could for the wedding.

Both Janet and Dave enjoyed the Church of the Open Door. The people there became their family away from home.

---

7 The Navigators is a worldwide Christian para-church organization. Its purpose is the discipling of Christians with a particular emphasis on enabling them to share their faith with others.

Dave Hears the Call to Mission Work

One day while Dave was at the Church of the Open Door, a missionary, Maver Roth, stopped by. Maver had just sent a load of lumber by rail to Cantwell, a small settlement at the junction of the Parks and Denali Highways. "I'm looking for a couple of men to help me build a little church at Cantwell," he said.

"I'd love to do that," Dave told him. But he'd spent all his leave time with his family and Jan and thought he couldn't possibly help the missionary. He left the church with his head hanging, only to be stopped by a sergeant with a lot of hash marks on his sleeve.

The officer had heard the exchange and said, "I've got a plan. You do what I tell you to do, and we'll pray." He told Dave to ask his company commander for advance leave to help build the church.

Dave asked his boss for seven days leave and told him why. The commander turned the air blue with his swearing. "Who do you think you are, asking for favors like this?" After he finished his tirade, Dave slunk away.

After several weeks went by, the commander called Dave in. He shook his head, waved a paper at Dave, and demanded, "Who do you know at headquarters?"

"No one," Dave said.

He thrust the paper at Dave. It held the requested leave and the reason for it.

"Get out of here," said the commander. "Have fun."

Dave caught the train to Cantwell. His first night there, it snowed in the night. He woke with the sun shining in his eyes and six inches of snow on the ground. His watch said two o'clock. *Oh, oh,* he thought. *My watch has stopped. I've overslept!* But everyone else in the house was still asleep, and the other clocks gave the same time, so he realized it really was just a couple of hours after midnight. He lay down again until 6:30 a.m. By then Maver Roth and the carpenter, Irwin Avron, were up and ready to go to work. In the meantime, the early June sunshine had melted all the snow.

For the next week, Dave worked as hard as he'd ever worked

THE STORY OF DAVE AND VERA PENZ

in his life. Workers started with the foundation, and by the end of the day the crew had the floor of the 24-by-40-foot building in place. The carpenter told Dave where to lay the shiplap lumber, then Dave nailed the boards down. The next day they put up the shiplap walls, and on the third day they installed the roof.

The three men spent day number four finishing the roof, working from 6:30 in the morning until 11:00 p.m. to take advantage of Alaska's long hours of summer daylight. While Dave worked, he felt God speaking to him about returning to Alaska as a missionary following his military service. Dave had been thinking hard about doing mission work somewhere. But the prospect of going back to school for training was difficult to deal with. He knew the key question was, "Am I willing to do what it takes to prepare for mission work?"

Several Native boys from the village, Gilbert and David Nikolai, along with two brothers named Stoney and Monson—all between 10 and 14 years old—hung around the worksite and watched. Up on the roof, Dave nailed boards in place, standing close to the edge so he could visit with the boys on the ground. He needed to trim a couple inches off a board to make it fit, but there was no place to lay it while cutting, so he held it between his legs. He sawed away at the end of the board, aware that God was speaking to him as he talked to the boys. While telling God that he was willing to be made willing to go to school, he forgot to watch the handsaw. When the end fell off the board, the saw blade hooked in Dave's pants and made an inch-long gash in his leg.

"God has a sense of humor," Dave said. "He made me sign that promise in blood. I've got the scar on my leg signifying I was willing to try school again. That was confirmation of my missionary call." And that call would lead to a lifetime of using his hands to serve the Lord.

Marriage, Illness, and Surgery

The summer passed quickly. Dave sold his airplane for $400,

and with what Jan had saved, the two were married on September 20, 1955. They spent the next few months in Anchorage.

Dave hadn't really been well since his illness soon after entering the Army. He was tired all the time, coughing phlegm and tissue out of his lungs. The Army doctors couldn't help. They gave him a statement of release to sign, and he was discharged in February 1956.

He and Jan moved back to Minnesota and bought a small mobile home to live in. Dave found a job managing the operations of a gravel pit, and they moved their trailer into the pit. He ran all the machinery and also taught Jan how to operate heavy equipment.

In the pit, sand was stockpiled higher than the house. Water filled the hole left by the sand and gravel dredging, making a popular place for young people to swim and party at night. Their screams and laughter kept Dave and Jan awake. In the morning Dave had to pick their beer cans out of the sand before he could load the trucks.

Finally, Dave came up with a plan. "Let's have some fun tonight," he said to Jan. "I'll take the shotgun. After the party gets going, you start screaming. I'll shoot the gun, and you quit in mid-scream."

He and Jan climbed the back side of the sand pile and watched at least a dozen kids with their cases of booze. Then they slid back down the pile about 50 feet, and Jan screamed, long and loud. Following Dave's gunshot, there was utter silence, then sounds of pandemonium as the kids scrambled for their vehicles, leaving the booze behind in their wild flight. Dave and Jan laughed so hard they could hardly walk home, and they had no more sleepless nights.

By the fall of 1956, Jan was several months pregnant, and Dave was sick again—so weak he could barely stand. He spent a week at the Mayo Clinic in Rochester. Doctors were determined to find out what was wrong with him. Using a scope, they found that his lung had collapsed from bronchiectasis. They said if they could remove the bad parts, perhaps the rest would heal. Dave told the doctors how he'd gotten sick in the Army and hadn't been well since. They contacted the Veteran's Administration, who sent a lawyer to see him. The lawyer and VA doctors checked out Dave's story and found it was true. The VA came back, promising to do everything in their power for him. But Dave said, "You had your turn. I'm only going to let the Mayo Clinic touch me from now on."

At that time, the usual surgery for his condition involved removing some ribs. However, in February, Mayo Clinic surgeons took out a large section of his lung using a new procedure where they spread the ribs apart so they could enter the chest cavity between them. It was a first for Mayo Clinic. Dave told people "It was like they opened me up with a can opener." He was left with a scar that went around his body from front to back, but he still had all his ribs.

While Dave recuperated in the hospital, Jan, by now six months pregnant with daughter Jeanne, was driving one day when she topped a hill on a narrow road and panicked when she saw a vehicle coming straight toward her. She wasn't able to pull over far enough, and in the ensuing head-on collision, her car radiator was smashed in. Fortunately, both Jan and the baby were all right.

Preparing to Answer the Call

During his six months of recuperation from the surgery, while Dave was unable to work, the call to missions was never far from his mind. He wondered if the enforced rest was an opportunity to pursue the call. "Let's take a look at Moody Bible Institute," he said to Jan. The school, founded in 1886 by famed evangelist Dwight L. Moody, was and still is a well-known Christian institution of higher education.

Dave and Jan drove from Rochester to Chicago to visit the school. Dave told administrators he was a pilot, knowing that skill was useful for missionaries in many parts of the world. At that time, Moody's aviation program had room only for jet pilots returning from the Korean conflict. Although Dave tested for the aviation program, his reading skills were so poor the teachers didn't think he could keep up in the classes. Also, his physical exam showed back problems.

"We don't want you to fly," officials said. "Most of our missionary pilots develop bad backs. It just wouldn't make sense to put you in a program like that." They suggested that he enter the program for regular missionaries.

So Dave registered for six weeks of summer school courses. Jan stayed behind in Minnesota while Dave attended summer school until their firstborn, Jeanne, arrived. In June 1957, Dave and Jan towed their trailer to Hammond, Indiana, which is south of Chicago. Freeways hadn't yet been built. Every morning they left home at six a.m. and drove the 20 miles to Moody along Lakeshore Drive. To Dave, the traffic was like being in a daily stock-car race, bumper to bumper at 50 to 60 miles per hour.

Dave loved Moody Bible Institute, but as he recovered from surgery, he realized that he couldn't pay their household bills and go to school too. He couldn't do the assignments fast enough to keep up in the regular classes, so he took night classes and worked during the day.

In his first job, he helped put cars together at a Ford assembly plant. As the unfinished vehicles passed on the assembly line, he welded in the trunk part of each car. Between vehicles, he worked on his school assignments until the next car arrived at his station.

In his next job, for Central Watch Alarm Company, he checked malfunctioning radar and ultrasonic alarms. He particularly enjoyed the work, because fixing the units took him to interesting places all over Chicago.

Daughter Valerie arrived in January 1959, while they still lived in the Chicago area. By June 1961, Dave had finished his night school missionary courses, and he and Jan were eager to begin missionary work. They felt drawn toward Arctic Missions, Inc., the group they'd become acquainted with in Alaska. John Gillespie, the pastor who had performed their wedding ceremony in

Anchorage, was now director of the ministry and lived in Portland, Oregon. They contacted him and signed up with that organization. Since Dave had had no experience in church leadership and was uncomfortable talking in front of an audience, Gillespie wanted them to have more experience in a church situation, so he asked Dave to think about a missionary internship.

But Dave wanted to be able to learn the language of the people he'd be working with. He hoped the Wycliffe Bible Translators' Summer Institute of Linguistics could help with that goal. Dave and Jan left their little girls with his parents and traveled to North Dakota for the six-week institute. But Dave discovered that the hearing loss he'd experienced as a youngster driving loud farm machinery left him unable to distinguish linguistic sounds well enough. Though Jan did well and he loved the program, no matter how hard he tried, he was unable to succeed. When the program ended, they both knew Dave couldn't be a translator.

Remembering John Gillespie's advice, they joined a Detroit-based missionary internship program designed to give internees practical experience in a church setting. They were sent to a rural church in a farming community near Lansing, Michigan, about 100 miles from Detroit, where they were assigned to help a pastor who had been saved in his late 40s. To Dave, Pastor Henry Bush seemed "rougher than a corn cob, a tough farmer kind of guy."

The two got along well. While they worked together jacking up the church building and installing foundation blocks beneath it, Dave told Henry, "I'd rather clean toilets than get up in front of people." Cleaning bathrooms and vacuuming the church became part of his job. But once a month he also had to preach the morning service. And every Monday the Penzes drove to a class in Farmington, Michigan.

Dave felt right at home as he visited with farmers and helped them with milking, butchering, and other chores. In fact, he loved it. Going into homes and spending time with the people was much like the work he hoped he'd be doing in Alaska.

CHAPTER 8
Cantwell

Off to Alaska

Their third child, Dianne, was born in November 1961. By then the Penzes had finished their internship and were eager to begin ministry in Alaska. But first they had to finish raising support. Throughout their training, they'd been talking to people about their call to Alaska.

When enough people had pledged support in finances and prayer, Dave, Jan, and their three little girls set off across the Lower 48 states and then up the Alaska Highway, a long, dusty drive. When it rained, the road turned to mire. It wasn't the easiest of trips. For one thing, five-year-old Jeanne and three-year-old Valerie got sick with an itchy rash that turned out to be measles. The family stopped for a few days in a hotel, and their mother bathed them with baking-soda water to soothe the itch. Because light hurt their eyes, Jan hung blankets over the windows. All was not misery, though. Jeanne remembers her father going out for a while and returning with a special treat—orange soda pop.

Further north along the highway, as they were driving through deep mud, the car suddenly slowed and came to a stop. Dave peered into the engine compartment, walked around the car, and finally looked underneath. He spotted the problem right away—no gas tank. He found it on the road, 300 feet behind them. The mud had pushed it from underneath the car. Dave jacked the car up in the mud and hung the tank back in place.

Baby Dianne was only a year old, still in cloth diapers. Once, the diaper was so messy that Jeanne remembers her mom saying, "I'm not going to keep that in the car!" And she heaved it as far as she could into the bushes along the road.

They finally arrived at Victory Bible Camp, at the base of the Talkeetna Mountains about 95 miles northeast of Anchorage, just in time for the scheduled missionary conference. All of the village missionaries for Arctic Missions, Inc. were there for their yearly week of fellowship. The leaders were surprised. No one had expected the Penzes to raise their support that quickly.

Return to Cantwell

The mission directors met with the Penzes and came up with an idea. "Remember the church at Cantwell? The missionary there needs to move to Florida because of his health. Would you take his place until we can find someone permanent?"

"We'll do it!" Dave exclaimed.

So the Penz family found themselves at the village along the Alaska Railroad where, seven years before, Dave had spent a week helping to construct the church building. Among the people greeting them were Gilbert, David, Stoney, and Monson—the boys Dave had been talking to when God called him to be a missionary. With the youngest of them now in their late teens, they became the core of the young people's group in the Penzes' first missionary assignment.

After the Penzes settled in at Cantwell, Dave heard about a former railroad section house for sale at Summit, about 10 miles away. Railroad maintenance supervisors once lived in section houses scattered along the rail line. Dave's imagination took flight. His interest in camps for village young people had been stirred when he first saw Victory Bible Camp. He said to his two oldest daughters, "Let's tear that building down. We'll use the lumber to build a Bible camp."

The Penzes' new community lay along the George Parks

Highway about halfway between Fairbanks and Anchorage. The Alaska Railroad tracks roughly paralleled the highway as they passed Cantwell, with the route's highest point, nearby Summit, at 2,363 feet above sea level.

The sturdy, three-story section house contained plenty of lumber. So with the occasional "help" of his little daughters, Dave worked all winter, taking the building apart from the inside out so they'd be protected from winter weather during most of the demolition. Dave recruited a team of men to fill two train cars with lumber. They sent the lumber to the town of Nenana, where some of it was used to build a bus barn next to missionary Russ Arnold's house. The barn would provide shelter for the school bus that Russ drove and kept at his home.

They loaded the remaining lumber on a barge and shipped it down the Yukon River to be used for the main building at Kokrine Hills Bible Camp, which had been Dave's goal when he bought the structure. This camp was also run by Russ Arnold.

The time that Dave and Janet spent at Cantwell's mission church became their pattern for the next four years. Because Dave was handy with tools, he made needed repairs on the homes of the missionaries they were filling in for. The rest of the time, the Penzes worked alongside villagers whenever they could, doing pretty much what the villagers did. They held Sunday school and children's meetings. At night, people came to their house to visit and ask questions.

Spiritism in the Villages

Missionaries need great patience and love as they try to bring God's truth to the villages. Alcoholism and abuse—both physical and sexual—are everyday realities for many residents. Many are spiritually starving, easily deceived, and trapped by animistic beliefs and fear of demons.

The Penzes soon learned that alcohol and demonic influence often go together. Once at Cantwell, a villager decided he was going to kill God, or failing that, Dave Penz, the man he considered to be God's representative in the village. Dave heard him coming down the road, screaming drunken invective. He had lost one shoe and was staggering toward their house, carrying tennis-ball-size rocks. The ground in that area was littered with rocks, providing a handy way for him to reload.

"I've got to head him off or he'll bust all the windows out of the house," Dave said to Janet.

Dave went to the road to meet the man and try to talk to him, but the man was out of his head with intoxication and demonic-fueled anger. He responded by throwing his rocks at Dave. Despite his condition, his aim was good, and several rocks hit their mark. In pain, Dave knew he had to get close enough that the drunk couldn't throw, but when Dave was within three feet of him, the man yanked his belt off and began to whirl its big buckle at Dave's head.

Dave could think only that he had to get the man on the ground, so he dove at his legs, knocked him down, and threw himself on top of the man's body. The drunk started to cry like a baby. About that time, some other inebriated men came along and offered to take their friend home, so Dave released him into their hands.

It's hard for many people in the United States to understand the reality of evil spirits in some cultures. The old shamanism in Alaska was often demonic in nature. Later, Dave came face to face with that demonic power again when he visited an upriver Indian village to attend a Stick Dance, a tradition still practiced by some Athabascans in Alaska and in the Southwestern United States. It is a dance and potlatch meant to honor the departed and help families deal with their loss. Dave thought he ought to attend as a learning experience.

Three or four men had gone into the woods to find just the right spruce pole, or "stick." They cut notches into it and attached objects that symbolized the deceased people. They brought the decorated pole into the community hall where all the guests were assembled and tied it to the ceiling so it stood upright. Drums beat slowly at first as men danced around the pole. The tempo increased and the drums got louder until they reached a crescendo. By then, the dancers circling the stick were no longer touching the floor. They were actually running in the air a foot above the floor. The hair on the back of Dave's neck stood up, and he felt the oppressive presence of many demons. He fled the hall as fast as he could.

Summer camps, no matter how primitive compared to those available in more privileged parts of the United States, gave young people hope. At camp they learned that God loved them and was stronger than demons. They learned that they were worthy of love and respect. But because demonic influence was so strong in some villages, when the kids came to camp, some of them heard voices at night. They saw objects move around by themselves, or they heard banging on the walls. They reported seeing little people running around inside their heads. Some children were so scared, they wanted candles burning all night. But when the campers put their trust in the Lord, those manifestations lessened.

Dave discovered a way to deal with the demons when a village woman called his friend Don, pleading, "What can I do? They're bothering me all the time." Don suggested that she read her Bible aloud in the morning and again at night and see what might happen.

The woman called back a week later and told Don, "They're gone! They don't like it when I read the Bible out loud."

Dave started suggesting that other Native people do the same thing. They found that it worked. "The demons hear what we say," Dave told them, "but they can't hear the thoughts in our head. They hate to hear God's Word, so they leave.

CHAPTER 9
Shageluk

Making a New Home Livable

In 1963, following the Penzes' year at Cantwell, mission supervisors asked them to fill in at Shageluk, a tiny village whose Ingalik Indian name means "village of the dog people." Some villagers told the Penzes the name also meant "rotten fish." Either name could describe a place where living was difficult.

The mission suggested that while the Penzes were at Shageluk, Dave could fix up the home they'd be living in. The previous missionary was gifted in many ways, but making repairs was not one of his talents. He'd started to build a log cabin, and although he didn't finish it, his family lived there anyway. They depended on an inefficient, homemade oil-barrel stove for heat, and in the absence of a kitchen sink, washed their dishes in a basin.

The Penz family loaded their belongings, along with many framed windows and other items from the torn-down Summit section house, onto a railcar. At Nenana, they unloaded the railcar and put everything onto a barge, built and operated by Native Alaskan David Maillelle. It had a powerful engine and was the only self-propelled barge in the area. Dave Penz considered the man a genius with engines and mechanical equipment. By taking a shortcut through the Holikachuk slough, Maillelle shortened the Penzes' 600-mile trip down the Yukon and up the Innoko River by 200 miles.

The Penzes' new home in Shageluk had only two windows. When

Dave and Jan stepped into the gloomy interior, they wondered what they'd gotten themselves into. But using a chainsaw, Dave cut new window openings in the log walls, then installed windows from the Summit section house all around the cabin.

Then he fashioned an improved stove out of two oil barrels. The one on the bottom held the fire. The stovepipe went through the top barrel that functioned as a heat saver. Instead of heat going out the chimney, hot air in the upper barrel radiated warmth throughout the cabin. The stove also heated water that Dave pumped into a barrel in the attic. Another barrel beside it held cold water. Voila! A gravity-fed system with hot and cold running water! Next, Dave installed a kitchen sink.

Janet sewed curtains and set about turning the cabin into a home. Although she had only a Coleman camp stove to cook with, she learned to bake one loaf of bread at a time using an empty five-gallon gas can, with the top cut out. She would put the bread pan inside the larger square can, cover the opening with foil, and set it on the burner.

After a while, they got a propane cookstove and installed propane lights. No longer was their bedtime dictated by when the sun went down.

Dave made other needed repairs, too. He and Jan painted the interior and began inviting their neighbors in for fellowship. Although it's usually hard for outsiders to find acceptance in Native villages, Dave and Jan's ebullience and love for the people helped them develop close relationships. A number of people came to know about the Lord because of their influence.

A Hunting Trip with Charlie

When the family arrived in Shageluk, they met a neighbor named Charlie, whose father had been a white prospector and his mother a Native. Charlie had a wife and three children, but because he was an alcoholic, he barely managed to keep food on their table. Often while Charlie was on a drinking binge, Dave would see the wife trying to haul firewood by herself, and he would go to help her.

One winter day Charlie said, "Dave, how about you go moose hunting with me? We can use your dogs, and I'll show you where to go." Although Charlie owned a couple of dogs, they were too scrawny to pull a sled.

So the men hitched up Dave's dogs to a sled and headed into a remote area where none of the villagers hunted. When they finally arrived and set up camp, the early dark of midwinter had fallen.

The next day, snow fell steadily while they spent the short daylight hours trudging through the woods, watching for game. Just at dusk they came upon six moose clustered together in a thicket. They shot two and then skinned and butchered them. They spread the pieces in the snow to freeze. By the time they finished, it was pitch dark and still snowing.

"I trap here, so I know this place," Charlie said. "I'll show you a shortcut back to camp."

Dave put a large chunk of meat in his backpack, picked up his heavy gun, and followed Charlie. He could barely see where they were going. They stumbled over fallen logs and sometimes fell elbow-deep in the snow.

When Charlie stopped moving forward, Dave asked, "What's wrong?"

Charlie mumbled that things didn't look right. Then he started off in a different direction. He changed direction several times.

The moose meat grew heavier and heavier, and so did Dave's gun. Exhaustion weighed down his limbs.

Charlie took the larger gun to carry and gave Dave his lighter one.

"Are you sure you know where we are?" Dave asked.

Charlie refused to admit they were lost. He said sarcastically, "Maybe you know which way to go."

Dave stood still for a few minutes, praying.

Suddenly he remembered that his flashlight might still be in his pack, and he rummaged through the contents until he found it. When Dave shone the light through the woods, they could see their own tracks circling around to where they stood. They were the only people within many miles, and Charlie couldn't deny any longer that they were lost.

While Dave repacked his belongings, he prayed aloud, asking God to help them find their way back to camp. Then he stood and watched snowflakes falling in the beam of his flashlight. They fell at a slight slant, telling him the wind blew from the north. He knew he had to go east to get to camp and the river. Dave started out in the lead this time. He plowed straight through the heavy, snow-covered brush and came to a frozen lake. They kept slogging eastward.

Now Charlie thought he heard noises behind them. "It must be wolves!" he said in a shaky voice. "They smell the meat you're carrying." He followed so close he kept stepping on Dave's heels. "Shine the light back there, Dave. See if it reflects from their eyes." Several times, Dave did so, but they saw no hungry wolves.

However, the last time Dave swung the flashlight around to the front again, he caught the faint impression of their sled tracks crossing the lake, covered by a foot of snow. Now Dave knew where their camp lay. They followed the tracks, shouting, and were soon greeted by the answering clamor of their sled dogs. They cooked and ate some of the moose meat Dave carried and fell exhausted into their sleeping bags.

The next day they took the dogs and sled back to where they'd left the meat. They were amazed to find one of the moose's long, heavy front legs a quarter mile away from the rest of the meat. A wolverine no doubt had helped itself and was probably not far away. The two men hung the leg in a tree, and Charlie set one of his traps beneath it.

Dave made several trips to get the meat and hides back to Shageluk, while Charlie stayed in the woods another night, hoping to catch the wolverine. The animal did come back for its prize and got caught in the trap.

Later, Dave told the story of the moose hunt in his sermons, pointing out to his listeners that most people don't know they are lost until they have the light of God's Word (like a flashlight) in their lives.

Sadly, Charlie failed to learn this lesson. He eventually died of alcoholism, never experiencing the illumination of God's Word.

Bringing in the Winter's Wood Supply

Living as their Native friends lived brought other adventures to the Penz family. Everyone in Shageluk used wood-burning stoves for heat and cooking. Wood was free and plentiful, if one went far enough away from the village to get it. In the fall, Dave and some villagers decided to work together to bring in their winter wood supply. They motored up a slough about 10 miles to where many dead white spruce still stood. Most were a foot in diameter at the base, nice and dry and easy to cut.

The woodcutters camped on the shore and began to fell the trees. They dragged 20-foot logs into the water and tied them together into a raft. They sawed other logs into shorter sections and piled them on the raft until they had a 20-by-20-by-6-foot stack. By the time they finished, it was evening, so they decided to spend one more night there.

The temperature dropped way below freezing that night, covering the slough with ice an inch thick. The woodcutters woke to find their boat frozen in place. They used poles to break the ice and clear a short path for the boat. Then Dave started the motor and proceeded to use the boat as an icebreaker, ramming it into the ice shelf.

To his surprise, instead of the ice breaking, it sheared through the bow of the boat like a knife. Water poured in. The men scrambled into the stern to lift the bow out of the water. Someone bailed frantically until they reached shore. They pulled the boat out of the slough, emptied it of water, and patched the hole. Then they motored down a running creek and returned to Shageluk.

Since the men's hard work remained frozen in increasingly thick ice, they had to look elsewhere for their winter's fuel supply. When Dave next flew over the spot, spring's high water had scattered the raft of wood. Not a stick could be seen anywhere.

Edison Hooley

The Penzes had heard about Edison Hooley, an intense young schoolteacher who also did missionary work among Native Alaskans. Dave and Ed became friends through their mutual interest in amateur (ham) radio.

Ed supported himself by teaching in the village schools but spent his summers sharing the Good News of the gospel. Knowing that people listen when they're sure you care about them, he was willing to do whatever he could to prove he did care.

One day, Ed Hooley landed his Cessna 140 on Shageluk's airstrip and walked over to the Penzes' house. "Hey, Dave, could you give me a hand at Holikachuk?" he asked. "The village keeps flooding out, so the people have decided to move to higher ground." He explained that villagers planned to tear their houses down, put them on barges, and haul them over to the largely abandoned village of Grayling, on the Yukon River. Holikachuk was only 25 or 30 miles from Shageluk, on the Innoko River, a tributary of the Yukon. Every summer, local villagers spent time at their summer fish camps on the Yukon, but low water in the Innoko made return trips difficult. Then during ice breakup in the spring, the opposite happened. High water would inundate the town.

Dave was happy to fly to Holikachuk with Ed and help the villagers dismantle some homes. He had recently built a new home in Holikachuk for Gale and Jeannie Van Diest, missionaries who later became the directors of Arctic Missions, Inc. Now he helped them tear down their new house and barge it and other homes, with the assistance of David Maillelle, to the site of Grayling. Then

Dave and Ed worked with the people to reassemble the buildings. Between 1962 and 1966, 25 families moved from Holikachuk.

During that time, the government sent workers to build an airstrip for the village, even though residents told them they were moving the town. After Holikachuk had been abandoned, someone camping on the site allowed a campfire to get away. The resulting blaze destroyed the remains of the town. Brush and trees soon grew over the unused airstrip.

Earthquake

By spring of 1964, the Penzes had finished work on the house in Shageluk while carrying on the work of the mission. Along with much of the rest of the state, Shageluk experienced a megathrust, 9.2-magnitude earthquake on March 27, the second most powerful quake ever recorded. Though it was centered in Prince William Sound near Valdez, shock waves caused great damage in Anchorage and other communities and rolled through distant Fairbanks. The communities of the Kuskokwim-Yukon Delta, hundreds of miles from ground zero, felt the earth rise and fall like waves on the sea.

Ernie Crabb, a missionary from Fairbanks, along with his son Doug, had flown in on a ski plane. They had just joined the Penzes for coffee when the log cabin began to rock. Clinging to the table, they turned their gaze toward the windows. They saw the ground outside roll in waves that seemed at least three feet high.

Throughout the affected area, people struggled to stand upright. A wave would roll under the trees, tilting them nearly to the ground on one side. Then they would spring upright and dip to brush the ground on the other side. Wave followed wave for several minutes, swinging the trees through an almost 180-degree arc.

When the ground stopped undulating, people checked on their neighbors. No one was hurt in Shageluk, and there was little damage beyond fallen stovepipes and toppled dishes. It took several days for reports of damage and fatalities in other parts of Alaska to filter through to the Lower 48 states because communication lines had failed. It was largely through the efforts of ham radio operators like Dave and Ed Hooley that the rest of the world learned what had happened in Alaska on that Good Friday.

Moving Shageluk

When ice jammed on the Innoko or water was high in the spring, Shageluk also frequently flooded, as Holikachuk had done. The Shageluk villagers decided to move, too. Dave told them about a spot he'd found at the foot of a south-facing hill. Because the south side of a hill gets more sunshine, it's warmer. The soil thaws sooner, and trees grow bigger. A lake in front of the site made it an ideal place for a village. But it was six miles away, and some villagers thought that was too far to go.

After the Penzes left in 1966, Shageluk residents also moved from their flood-prone location to a higher, north-facing site three miles downriver. The Bureau of Indian Affairs constructed 20 homes and a school at the new village. The mission built a new house there for the missionaries who came after the Penzes. But those who chose the site ignored the facts that permafrost lay under the ground's surface and not much timber was available nearby. Even today, residents must haul treated well-water for use in their homes. They have electricity, but no house is fully plumbed, so they use the village washeteria for laundry, bathing, and water. There are few paying jobs in the village, so some residents opt to look for work in Fairbanks or Anchorage.

Disruptions to Native Cultures

Exodus also happened for a number of other reasons in many Alaskan villages, both large and small. Before Europeans came, many Native people lived along Alaska's rivers. Now, Shageluk is the only Athabaskan community on the 600-mile length of the Innoko.

Those European newcomers brought smallpox and measles. Since the Native peoples had no immunity to those diseases, hundreds of families, sometimes whole villages, were wiped out. In the late 1800s, when thousands of miners rushed to the gold fields, many traveled up the Innoko River, bringing disease with them. About the same time, a variety of missionaries also came to Alaska. Denominations often staked their claims to areas, such as the Catholic and Episcopalian priests who divided between them the Athabaskan villages along the rivers east of the Kako area.

When the flu pandemic of 1918 hit Alaska, many children orphaned by influenza were sent to live at the missions. More Native traditions were disrupted, leaving people vulnerable to the worst that the supplanting culture had to offer.

This part of the history of Alaska's Native peoples—along with the harsh climate, vast distances, and cultural factors—helps to explain why it's been particularly hard to reach them with the Good News of the gospel. But people of good will continue to reach out to help Native Alaskans become a vibrant, growing sector of Christ's worldwide church.

Chapter 10
Grayling, Kaltag, and Stony River

Grayling

After the 1964 Good Friday earthquake, the mission asked the Penzes to leave Shageluk and work in Grayling on the Yukon River. They loaded their belongings and their three little girls, ages four, six, and eight, onto a boat to join the Holikachuk families and other villagers already living there. During the year they spent in Grayling, Dave reconstructed the house he'd first built at Holikachuk for the regular missionaries, Gale and Jeannie Van Diest. By now the two older Penz daughters were in school with other village children. As always, the Penz family joined in community life as much as possible. They welcomed neighbors to their home for evening visits and also held Bible studies and kids clubs.

As in most Native communities, the villagers lived a subsistence lifestyle. They depended on fishing, hunting, trapping, and berry gathering. Few paying jobs were available beyond those at the store, the clinic, or the school, although some people had seasonal jobs, such as fighting wildfires.

Although local citizens had voted to exclude alcohol sales in the village, that didn't mean people couldn't still get alcoholic beverages. But the exclusion in "dry" villages meant better living for more people.

When the Penzes arrived, Grayling and its two neighboring villages of Shageluk and Anvik were nominally Episcopalian, but most people didn't understand the change that believing in Christ could make in a person's life. Priests instructed people not to listen to Dave. Most villagers didn't want to risk being ostracized by the church and their neighbors, although one of them, Walter Maillelle—David Maillelle's father—became a vibrant example of someone who dared to stand up for Christ.

Walter was a natural leader and well-loved by the people. People listened to him. When villagers abandoned Holikachuk and moved to Grayling, Walter organized a logging project to make lumber for new homes. He supervised about 15 men, one of whom was Dave, who worked hard and efficiently to cut 500 logs and pile them on the beach. When government officials saw the villagers' initiative, they were eager to give them other assistance. However, the storekeeper, Henry Deacon, later said that this government generosity led to some people desiring the material things of life rather than spiritual things.

Walter, though, had questions about spiritual matters. Often he would phone the Penzes after the other villagers had gone to bed and ask if he could come play dominos. He didn't want other Natives to know what they were really talking about. When Walter arrived, the Penzes would get out dominos and spill them on the table. Then they'd sit talking about God's Word. Walter was finally convinced of the truth of the Word and decided to follow Christ. But when he shared the gospel with other villagers, they turned on him and kicked him out of the community. Walter and his family moved to Anchorage. There he became a leader of Anchorage New Life Fellowship, ministering to Alaskan Natives in the city and through media broadcasts.

Walter was a humble man. Dave often saw him leading Bible studies and other meetings while kneeling on the floor. One man who knew about Walter's involvement in Native New Life Fellowship wrote,

I remember his love for God and people. One Sunday he

slipped $20 to me in a handshake. As I stood stunned (keep in mind back in 1979, $20 was a lot of money), he said, "God told me." He was always to me a very cool guy with a heart for listening as God led him.

Former Alaska Wycliffe translators Dave and Kay Henry, who later spent a number of years with InterAct Ministries in Yakutsk, Russia, knew the Maillelles well. They wrote of Walter:

> God used him as a great leader to get Anchorage Native New Life started. We remember several times when he brought a group of Natives to Fairbanks. We especially remember when he and his faithful wife, Virginia, with several Natives from the Anchorage area, came to our log cabin where we hosted them as they had a wonderful meeting of fellowship and sharing God's love with Fairbanks Natives! . . . He even came to Russia with InterAct to begin the work there. We, the Russian and Yakut people, are also thankful that he and others came to begin the work in Russia.

In 2000, Walter died in Anchorage at the age of 69. He left a heritage of humble service to the God he loved.

Kaltag

Following their year in Grayling, the Penzes moved in 1965 to Kaltag, located 97 miles up the Yukon River on the old portage trail that led through the mountains to Unalakleet on Norton Sound. It had been a trade route between the Athabascans of the Interior and the Eskimos on the coast. The people there were Koyukon Athabascan Indians who used to travel seasonally from camp to camp, following the migrations of wild game and fish. Kaltag itself, sitting on a 35-foot bluff at the base of the Nulato Hills, was once used as a cemetery for surrounding villages. In

1900, a shortage of food plus a measles epidemic killed a third of the area's Native population. Survivors from three nearby seasonal villages came together to regroup, and at that time the village of Kaltag was established.

The village had an airstrip. Other transportation was by snowmobile, dogsled, or—during the summer—riverboat. As in the other villages where the Penzes served, the temperature variations could be extreme—as high as 90 degrees in the summer and as low as minus 55 degrees in the winter.

When the Penzes came to Kaltag, the villagers were all Catholic, but Dave and Jan found ways to build bridges. They had seen how Ed Hooley used his small plane in ministry, and Dave desired to do the same. He heard of a plane for sale in Unalakleet, on Norton Sound. He rode the mail plane to Unalakleet. The Native pilot, Wilfred Ryan, invited him to stay with his family while Dave looked at the small plane, a PA12. He purchased it for $2,700, but before he could fly it home, a storm blew in, and he was stuck in Unalakleet for nine days.

The townspeople were evacuated to a large gymnasium on a hill because fierce onshore winds blew in seawater, filled with huge chunks of ice, flooding and battering homes. Dave evacuated, along with the Ryan family. When the storm ended, Dave went to see if his new plane had survived. Water had reached above the wheel wells, but didn't damage the engine. An iceberg large enough to crush the plane rested only six inches from the tail.

The Native people were impressed that Dave now owned a plane of his own, and more than once the aircraft proved to be a lifesaver. When a frantic message came in from the bush that a baby was dying of diarrhea-caused dehydration, Dave flew to the home in 40-below-zero temperatures, loaded up the sick child and its mother, and brought them back to Kaltag. Due to the frigid weather, however, the air breather in the oil vent froze up and caused the propeller seal to blow out. Most of the motor oil sprayed out over the windows so Dave couldn't see through the windshield. He had to use the side window to find his way back to Kaltag where a larger plane waited to fly his passengers on to the hospital in Fairbanks.

This incident proved to the villagers that Dave really did care about them, and their attitude toward him changed. But the loss of oil had ruined the motor. Though it cost a lot of money, Dave had it rebuilt, and God continued to use the plane and Dave's flying skills for the rest of the year they were at Kaltag.

When river ice broke up that spring, an ice jam formed and flooded the upriver village of Nulato. People had to camp outside in tents on the snow and ice while their homes dried out. This was especially hard on the elderly people, who began to get sick. When Dave got word of the situation, he made several trips to Nulato, ferrying the elders to Kaltag, where villagers took them in and kept them warm until the visitors could go home again.

Jeanne and Valerie Penz attended public school with the village kids. Nine-year-old Jeanne would set up the flannel board in their home, ready to tell stories when school let out. Thirty or 40 kids would come running down the trail to the Penzes' house, which couldn't hold them all. Children listened at the door and windows while Jeanne taught them stories from the Bible. If kids misbehaved, they had to put their name on a list on the door, and couldn't come inside for a week. The kids really wanted to hear the stories, so it didn't take long for them to settle down.

In the summer, Dave used his plane to fly the Kaltag children to a camp started by Gale Van Diest, the missionary who had worked at Holikachuk. When the Van Diests later moved to Grayling, Gale started the Grayling Creek Children's Camp. It was near the site where the airstrip was later built.

Stony River

As time for the Penzes' furlough neared, Arctic Missions, Inc. asked Dave and Jan if they would work at the Kuskokwim River village of Stony River for their next assignment. More than 200 miles south of Kaltag, it had a population at that time of fewer than 100 people. Most villagers were there because the federal government had decided that all Native children must have access to free public education. Eskimos from downstream on the Kuskokwim, plus Athabascan Indians speaking two separate dialects from up the Kuskokwim and Stony Rivers, were compelled to move to the village so there would be enough children to warrant building a school. No one village "chief" or elder was accepted by everyone. Old conflicts rose again between the Native cultures.

The Penzes knew the work there would be challenging, but they accepted the assignment. First, they would take their furlough. For that, they needed a car to drive down the Alaska Highway and on to Minnesota. Dave sold his plane and bought a vehicle.

While in Minnesota, Dave looked for a better plane to use in Alaska. His father talked with a man selling a nice, low-air-time Cessna 180. He asked only $6,000. Dave went to see it, although he let the seller know that he didn't have that much money. The man told him, "Pay me half now and the rest as it comes in."

"I'll try," Dave replied. He let various groups know the need as he and Jan spoke about their mission. In just a few weeks, he returned to the plane's owner with half the purchase price. He flew the plane away, and when the family returned to Alaska, they left the car behind and rode in the Cessna 180.

For their new assignment in Stony River, they rented a little log house. Dave installed water and sewer lines in it, then flew their belongings to their new community. Jeanne got to ride along with the first load. Once they landed, she walked around the village with her dad, getting acquainted with some of the neighbors. They were both so excited they forgot to eat lunch. When the two returned to their new home about five o'clock, Jeanne began to cry. She had no idea why she was crying, but her dad realized she was probably hungry. Rummaging through the supplies they'd brought in the plane, he found a large can of peaches. He opened it with his jackknife, and father and daughter ate the can's entire contents. She felt better right away and never forgot how good the peaches had tasted.

Since regular beds couldn't be carried in the small plane, Dave built wooden loft-type bunks along the walls of the children's bedroom. The beds were high enough to keep the children off the cold floor in winter and had storage room underneath.

In summer, the Penzes planted a big garden near the house. They heaped fertile soil into raised rows so the sun could better warm the plants' roots.

The family lived in Stony River for five years, from 1965 to 1970. Dave used the community as the base for his work, flying to surrounding villages (Lime Village, Sleetmute, Crooked Creek, Georgetown, and Red Devil) to visit people and share the love of Christ. He visited the people and showed Christian movies, distributed Sunday school papers, and sold or gave away books. Sometimes one of their children went along. Jeanne was thrilled to drop *Sunday Pix,* a weekly Christian comic book, out of the plane as they flew over a friend's house in Red Devil. At Sleetmute, she got to meet the schoolteachers, who later became Christians. Whenever Dave caught up with work at home, he'd fly to another village and get acquainted with the residents there.

At Stony River, as in other places they'd lived, Dave and Jan kept their house open to their neighbors. They held Good News Clubs and Sunday school and engaged in camp work. Sometimes they were even called upon to provide medical treatment, such as the time Dave was asked to deliver a baby. They'd help with first-aid for injuries and sometimes fly people to the hospital. Sometimes the village health aide would leave supplies with the Penzes when he or she had to be gone. They gave disease-prevention shots to children and antibiotic shots to those who contracted pneumonia.

In his spare time, Dave continued to work on his ham radio license. At that time, candidates for the license had to learn Morse code well enough to copy it at 13 words per minutes. They needed to learn electronic information as well. Finally, while in Stony River,

Dave passed the examination. He got his own radio equipment and built a transmitter. He could talk to people all over the state, even in the Lower 48, and sometimes at night he responded to calls from people in Russia or other faraway places. The family had no telephone, but Dave could ask another ham radio operator to patch him through to a phone if a call was necessary.

When the family moved to Stony River in 1967, the girls were six, eight, and 10 years old. Then, to everyone's delight, Jan became pregnant again. Three weeks before her due date, Dave flew Jan to Soldotna where they waited for the baby's birth. Jan's mother came from Minnesota to stay with her granddaughters, the first time in 46 years she had been away from their grandpa. She flew to Anchorage, and then to McGrath, where Dave picked her up to fly to Stony River. The girls had a wonderful time with their grandmother, who had no trouble with the challenges of village life. She'd always burned coal and corncobs in her stove on the farm, so getting used to the wood stove was not a problem.

The children and their grandmother listened every night to the "Ptarmigan Telegraph" broadcast from Nome, as messages went out to people all over the bush. Finally they heard the one they were waiting for, "To Grandma and girls in Stony River: It's a boy! Mother and baby are doing fine."

A brother! The girls screamed and jumped with joy. When baby Jonathan was two days old, Dave flew him and his mother home to the log cabin in Stony River. His big sisters warmly welcomed the baby boy.

Around this time their dad flew in two bikes for Jeanne and Valerie. The bikes made a big hit with the village kids who constantly begged to ride them. The Penzes realized that, while their children were an important part of their ministry, the girls needed to learn the balance between sharing and taking care of one's own property. Jan wisely told her daughters that when someone wanted to borrow a bike, it was permissible to say, "Not this time. Maybe next time."

Spiritual Warfare

In their interactions with people in the villages, including those in Stony River, the Penzes learned how to deal with the occult by pleading the blood of Jesus and praying in Christ's name. Dave said that non-Native people thought they were nuts if they talked about such experiences, but the demons were very real. They caused people to do wicked things they never would have done ordinarily, especially when alcohol was involved.

As had happened in Cantwell a number of years earlier, one evening a man who had been drinking heard demonic voices telling him to "kill God." While Dave was away, this man pushed his way into their house with his rifle. He made Jan and the children line up, then he faced the door, ready to shoot Dave when he came in. Jonathan, not yet three, didn't understand what was happening and wouldn't stay in line, so the man hit him with the butt of the gun until Jonathan obeyed him.

When Dave came home after dark, he realized someone was sitting in the grass outside, smoking. It was the man's sister. "Don't go in there," she said. "He's drunk and he's waiting to kill you."

Dave crept onto the covered porch. The door was open a crack and Dave saw that although everyone was lined up, they weren't being cooperative. They'd distracted the drunk and he'd turned his back to the door. Dave grabbed the closest thing at hand to use as a weapon. It happened to be a toy ax.

Dave slipped through the door and hit the man over the head with it. He fell to the floor. The rifle flew from his hand. Jan grabbed it while Dave tied the man's hands and feet.

Then he called a trooper at Bethel to come and get the man. The trooper refused to come because he didn't think it was serious enough, so Dave used his ham radio to call the trooper's boss in Anchorage. The officer in charge gave the Bethel trooper a good chewing out. He came as soon as the weather allowed and took the intruder to the Bethel jail.

While waiting for the officer, the Penzes kept the man bound in their house until he sobered up. He later apologized for his actions.

Another incidence of demonic influence happened when the Penz family had moved out of their first house in Stony River, although some of their belongings were still inside. Two men heard demons telling them to burn the missionaries' house. So they got two five-gallon cans of diesel fuel, broke windows in the house, and poured the fuel inside. Then they set it on fire. The men were caught and admitted their guilt. Their defense was that demons told them to do it. They were supposed to build a new cabin to replace the burned one, but no one ever followed through to make sure they did it.

In places so full of spiritual darkness, it's slow, hard work to bring people to a place of trust in Jesus Christ. Also, it's very important among Native Alaskans to fit in. If a person stands out in ambition or giftedness or chooses a different way of life, he or she is criticized and sometimes ostracized. When people do accept Christ, they may face opposition from family and neighbors. It's very difficult to stand up to that kind of pressure, so there's a great need for discipleship training as well as Christian fellowship.

One thing the Penzes tried to do with their converts was to teach them about spiritual warfare. Dave led one of the Stony River elders, Iyana, to the Lord, and taught him how to invoke the blood of Jesus in prayer. He'd been a strong leader in the village. When he was saved, he quit drinking and never touched liquor again. He was determined to persuade the other villages to do the same and talked to them frequently about it. But in spite of his former standing, they refused to listen to him. Nevertheless, Iyana stayed faithful until his death. He knew that people might not listen, might even think he was crazy, but only God could know the influence his life would have.

Dave had proof of this one night when he saw two drunken young men fighting over a snow machine. They were screaming at each other, so drunk they could hardly stand erect. He sent up a quick prayer for wisdom and walked over to see if he could help. When he got there, they said, "We're okay, Dave. We're just having fun."

Dave tried to talk to them, but they both bent over at the waist and kept their eyes on the ground. Suddenly sobered, they forgot all about their argument.

"What's the matter with you guys?" Dave asked.

Dave realized they must be seeing the presence of God in his life when they said, "You're too bright. We can't look at you. The light hurts our eyes!"

CHAPTER 11
Ministry in the Bush

Camp Inowak

One day, Dave flew downriver from Stony River to the village of Sleetmute. About halfway between the two villages he spotted a large gravel bar in the river, the perfect size for landing a small plane. Nearby lay an oxbow lake, formed when the river moved into a new channel. Dave realized that an area beside the U-shaped lake could become a wonderful campsite. He immediately visualized tents and buildings with happy kids splashing in the water and doing all the other things kids do at camp. The site was isolated, 18 miles by riverboat from Stony River, but that was not a drawback in Alaska.

In the summer of 1968, Camp Inowak, "The Place Where the River Comes Out," became a reality. Dave and some of the villagers built a 12-by-14-foot main cabin and set up surplus army tents for campers to sleep in.

When Dave asked, the village moms and dads said, "Sure, you can take our kids." So he loaded them into the plane, two per seat, landed on the gravel bar, then took them by boat up a slough to the lake and on to the camp. He could fly only six at a time, so it took many trips to get all the children there, then home again. Though he carried $1 million worth of insurance in 1968, no regulations had been put into effect yet specifying only one passenger to a seat.

The village kids arrived starved for love and attention, and many responded to the love they received at camp by putting their trust in Christ.

The first camp lasted for two weeks. The next years' camp sessions went on for three weeks, and finally so many young people wanted to come, they held camps for four weeks.

The village women asked Dave, "Why can't we have camp?" So women's camp was started with about 40 attendees from different villages.

The following March, the village men said, "You have camps for the kids and the women. How about us guys?"

"Great! We'll do it. How about a snow camp?"

So the men rode their snow machines down the frozen river and, as Dave described it, "had a blast" at camp.

When the fourth busy summer of camping began, one of the fathers asked, "Dave, did you ever think of having a family camp?"

Dave pondered a few minutes. Then he responded, "Tell everybody to bring their tents on the Fourth of July weekend, and we'll have a family camp." So they did.

Staff members were local people, as well as volunteers from churches in Alaska and in other states. The role of the counselors, as in any youth camp, was simply to befriend the kids, joining with them in various camp activities and as opportunities came up, to share their faith in Christ. The activities eventually included swimming, riflery, archery, box hockey, and a zip line.

Among those helping were Ed Hooley, the schoolteacher who spent his summers and weekends flying to assist missionaries in the area. Ed had already begun to think about establishing a kids' camp at his Kako gold-mine site, the first step in fulfilling his dream of providing fellowship opportunities for Christian adults in the far-flung communities.

Camp Inowak conditions and equipment were primitive but well adapted for the setting. The camp kitchen consisted of pole framework covered with plastic sheeting. It had a plank floor, with a wooden serving counter along one side. Dave installed a stove, a sink with running water, and work surfaces. Ruby Gaede, the well-loved camp cook, could roll up the plastic wall at mealtimes. Campers lined up outside along the counter to get their meals.

One of the tents housed a homemade wooden bathtub lined with Visqueen. After the kids went home on Saturdays, the staff filled it with water heated over the fire and took their baths. More than one person had to use the same water, but they didn't mind. At least they were able to get cleaner than they'd been.

Camp Inowak was located in bear country. Because bears passed close by the camp on their way to the river, the staff brought dogs along. At night they tied them near the bear trails so they'd bark if the bruins came near.

One night Dave heard their dog, Tullus, ki-yiing in terror. He leaped up, and in his skivvies, stepped outside the sleeping quarters. Tullus strained at the end of his tether, backed up as far as the chain allowed. A black bear sat facing the dog, reaching out occasionally to tap him on the nose.

Dave ran across the open space between the sleeping quarters and the pole-and-Visqueen kitchen building, where his gun was hanging from a nail stuck in a pole. Unaware that the curious bear was trotting behind him, he grabbed the gun off the nail and cocked it. He felt the touch of a leathery nose on bare skin and heard a snuffle. He swung and shot from the hip. The seven-foot bear reeled back, then ran all the way around the cabin before collapsing at his feet, dead. Dave had shot it right through the heart.

A Lesson in Yielding

One windy February day, Dave flew from Stony River to the nearby village of McGrath, the transportation and economic hub for that part of Western Alaska. He planned to pick up Jan, who'd been in Anchorage buying groceries and other supplies. In Jan's care was a 10-year-old Yupik girl, Lisa Carpenter.

Dave's plane, a Piper PA-12 Super Cruiser, was the single-engine workhorse flown by many bush pilots. High winged, it had a single seat in front for the pilot and a wider seat in back for passengers. Since it was difficult in those days to keep snow cleared from bush airfields, all pilots used skis on their small planes in the winter. The skis on Dave's plane were held in place by 3/16-inch stainless steel cables running from the back and front of each ski and bolted to the landing gear.

After most of the boxes and bags were loaded into the plane, Jan and Lisa situated themselves in the backseat, while Dave handed in the rest of the baggage to tuck around their feet, behind their heads, and on their laps. When everything and everyone had been packed in tightly, Dave climbed into the pilot's seat and took off into the wind. They'd climbed to about 100 feet when they heard and felt a sudden *ka-chunk*! The plane yawed sharply to the left.

Dave looked out the right window. When he saw nothing unusual, he looked out the window next to him and saw that the front of the left ski was dangling vertically. The bolt holding it had snapped, but the back cable prevented the ski from flipping upside down. The cable was about three feet outside the window and below it. The top of the ski was rounded, so Dave realized that if he could get it to flip all the way over, he could safely land the plane. But if he tried to land with the ski hanging as it was, the plane would surely cartwheel and, with its full gas tanks, burst into flame.

While flying with full right rudder to keep the plane straight, he prayed frantically, "Lord, what do I do?" and then radioed the controller at McGrath.

"I'll call out the fire trucks and crash people," the controller told him.

Meanwhile, Dave struggled to keep the plane's velocity at about 80 miles per hour, because faster or slower speeds caused the aircraft to bump and jerk. While he focused on that task, the wind was tossing the plane up and down and from side to side.

Because of the snow and cold, Dave had used duct tape to seal all the openings in the plane. Now he struggled to peel the tape from around the left window so he could slide it open and lean his head out. Then he stuck his arm out but couldn't reach the cable holding the ski. Frigid wind poured into the plane while Jan prayed hard. She and Lisa pulled sleeping bags around themselves.

Dave called back to Jan, "I need to try cutting this cable. Can you get my tools out from underneath that stuff in the back? There's a pair of wire cutters in there."

Jan twisted in her seat and dug through the pile of baggage until she reached the toolbox. She found a pair of wire cutters and handed them to Dave.

Dave held the control yoke between his knees, keeping the plane level and steering with his legs. Reaching out the window, he closed the cutters around the back cable, but the cable was too thick to sever. He gave up and looked around the airplane for something to use to pull the cable close enough to grab. Then he saw an old gun that had a hook on its front side. He used the hook to snag the cable and pull it within reach.

"Give me the hacksaw, Jan."

Jan handed him a hacksaw from his toolkit. Ordinarily, that would have cut the cable easily, but with the powerful wind jerking and pushing both cable and hacksaw, Dave couldn't hit the same spot twice. He gave up on that too.

Joking comments came over the radio's loudspeaker on the ceiling. "Hey, we're getting cold out here. Hurry up and crash!"

Someone on the ground suggested, "Why don't you try to stub that toe on the ground and break the ski and gear off?

"How would that work?" Dave asked.

"The last guy who tried it, the ski and gear came off and went through the backseat where the passengers sat."

That didn't sound good to Dave, but no one could think of a better way. By this time, many of McGrath's 400 villagers had crowded along the runway to watch the drama. Dave had been praying, "Lord you got me this airplane. You've kept us here in Alaska all these years." But he was not willing to say, "Okay, Lord, if you want us to burn up in a ball of fire, that's up to you." He knew the situation was extremely serious, but he also knew that he needed to get to the place where he could tell God he was willing to die.

By now, the plane had been circling the airstrip for nearly 45 minutes. He'd used up much of the gas in the tanks, but still he struggled with letting go and letting God take over. Finally, he gave up. "Okay, God, I'm out of ideas. It's up to you. If it's our time to die, that's okay, too."

He looked back over his shoulder to Jan, who had her arm wrapped around Lisa. "I'm going to try one more thing," he shouted. Steering the plane south, away from the town, he slowed the speed and tried to push the back of the ski down. It didn't budge. His glance fell on the gun beside him. An impossible thought popped into his head. "I'll shoot that cable off!"

With a rush of adrenaline, he rummaged around the crowded cockpit and found some bullets. In his excitement, while loading the gun, he inadvertently poked its barrel right into the loudspeaker and broke it. He didn't realize until later what he'd done.

Thrusting the gun out the window, he aimed it at the bouncing wire. He pulled the trigger, but missed. The gun sight was at least half an inch above the hole in the barrel. "That's not gonna work," he told himself. "I'll have to put the gun right on the wire."

He shoved the gun outside the window again and put the end of the barrel right on the cable. With his hand on the stock, his finger down as far as he could reach, he squeezed the trigger. The cable cut cleanly. The ski flipped over so the longer part dragged to the back. Now all they had to do was land on one good ski and one upside-down ski. Instead of sliding on the ground on a long ski, he figured the plane should slide smoothly along the ice on the rounded hump that remained.

Jubilant watchers came running as the plane touched down on

McGrath's airstrip. Dave shut off the engine, hoping the propeller wouldn't slash people swarming the plane. Amidst the shouted congratulations, Dave tried to get the passengers out of the plane. Jan couldn't find her glasses.

"Look behind the seat. Maybe you put them in the pocket," Dave told her.

Just then the crowd of people lifted the left side of the plane so they could swing the ski right side up. As the seat came up to meet Jan, she exclaimed, "Oh, I'm fainting,"

Lisa giggled and pointed to the people lifting the plane.

While a mechanic repaired the cables, friends took them to their house for coffee. Dave's hands shook so hard he couldn't hold his cup still. In the midst of his friends' razzing, he could think only of the lesson he'd just learned, the bottom line in any life situation: "Are you willing to let God do what he wants to do?

Soldotna, McGrath, and Anchorage

The Penzes' continued their involvement in Camp Inowak for about 15 years, although after five years in Stony River, the family moved to Soldotna so the girls could attend high school. Soldotna, a town on Alaska's Kenai Peninsula, was where the Missionary Aviation Repair Center (MARC) was headquartered. When the Penzes moved there, Dave went to work for MARC with the understanding that he was free to travel to the villages anytime he needed to. It didn't work out that way, though. As soon as he got one plane repaired, where was always another one that needed work. He found himself so busy fixing planes on the ground, he didn't get to fly much.

He stayed with MARC for a year, then told his employers he'd decided to go to McGrath on the Kuskokwim River. McGrath, whose population was two-thirds white and one-third Native, had a good high school, and Dave hoped to start a work there for Native people from the villages.

He spent the summer in McGrath building a house to live

in. Hoping to host Bible classes there for Native people from the villages, he built the house large enough to hold those who would come.

Meanwhile, Jan struggled with many of the issues that missionaries face—the isolation, being so far away from her family in Minnesota, trying to raise children in a different culture, worrying about how locals perceived their new house. In Native cultures, you don't "try to act big" or do things that seem to draw attention to yourself, so Jan wondered if the new house, the largest in the village, might be at counter purposes to their ministry. She tried hard to hide her struggles but became so depressed that Dave realized she needed to get away from Alaska for a while.

By now, the Cessna 180 he'd been flying for a number of years needed a new engine. The people at MARC suggested that he take a midwinter break and go to the Lower 48 states for a couple of months. MARC could put a new engine in the plane during this time.

The Penzes asked neighbors to watch the new house for them, and the family flew to Minnesota. They stayed with Jan's family for half a year, December through June. It helped Jan's state of mind immensely.

That winter the snow piled to five feet deep around their house in McGrath. Neighbors didn't notice when one dark night an inebriated man kicked in the door and slept off his drunk in the Penzes' upstairs bedroom. Still woozy, he lit a cigarette and dropped it on the bed. He left, but the cigarette smoldered until the bed caught fire, burned through the floor and fell down into the kitchen. By the time someone saw the smoke, the house was gutted. Village firefighters had just returned from a program where they'd learned about fighting fires where basic amenities, such as fire trucks and hydrants, were often missing. They flooded the floor of the house with half an inch of water, then beat on the outside walls. That caused ashes and embers to fall from the ceiling into the water and create steam. The steam thus created snuffed out the fire. Although they saved the outside walls, everything inside was destroyed.

Since it would take another six months for the house to be made livable, Dave and Jan decided to stay in Minnesota another year. That way, the kids wouldn't have to change schools again mid-year. They moved to a mobile home on property belonging to Dave's brother. Not everything was wonderful for the family, but the kids loved having time with their cousins. With the longer stay, members of the visiting missionary family were treated less like VIPS than on their usual furloughs. The kids got to see what normal life in the Lower 48 was like, and, according to daughter Jeanne, that was healthy for them.

When the year was up, the family returned to Alaska. The Penzes' work at McGrath was planned to be an itinerant ministry, depending on a plane to get to the surrounding villages. But when the family arrived in Anchorage, they found their plane still hadn't received its new engine. Since their income as missionaries was low, and since MARC had offered to do the work, Dave had depended on them to do it for free, or at least cheaply. But MARC had to do paying jobs first, and they'd been so busy, they hadn't yet gotten to Dave's plane.

Since they could not carry out their planned ministry at McGrath without an airplane, Dave and Jan went to work as facilitators for Arctic Missions Inc., replacing missionary John Van Wingerden, who'd had to move to a warmer climate because of his health. The family settled into the mission's house in Anchorage and provided hospitality for missionaries and Natives coming in from the villages, worked with Anchorage Native New Life, and purchased and sent needed items to AMI missionaries. Jan also did bookwork for AMI. She loved Anchorage, but Dave felt frustrated in town. He longed to be back in the bush. However, as he spent time working at the hospital with Natives who came for treatment, the experience inspired a desire to continue that work someday after retirement.

Among the missionaries the Penzes worked with in Anchorage were old friends Ed and Joyce Hooley. The goals and friendship they shared with the Hooleys would soon change the course of their lives.

CHAPTER 12
Mining, Mourning, and Ministry

The First Miners at Kako

After gold-rush fever subsided across the Klondike and Alaska, some miners continued to find gold in places like Alaska's Yukon-Kuskokwim (Y-K) Delta. In 1919, a prospector discovered gold on Buster Creek, about one mile from the present airstrip at Kako. (In the Native Yupik language, "Kako" means *clay*, or *place where clay is found*.)

The prospector hacksawed a two- or three-inch pipe lengthwise down the middle, fastened it back together, and pounded it into the creek bed. When he pulled it up and separated the halves, the pipe was packed with sand and gravel, which he panned in the creek. Tiny, glittering specks of gold flecked the black sand left in the pan. He excitedly filed four consecutive claims along a mile of Buster Creek. A couple of other families joined him, built cabins, and lived and worked at Kako until about 1930.

Below Buster Creek, three smaller creeks ran into Kako Creek. On Montezuma Creek, the Smith family built a home and did mining; other miners worked on Bobtail and Windy Creeks. They used picks, shovels, and wheelbarrows to dislodge the pay dirt and haul it to sluice boxes, where they ran water over the dirt to carry away the waste. The heavier gold dust settled out in the bottom of the sluice boxes behind the riffles, or crosswise slats, for later clean-up.

The first miners found the area to be rich in the precious metal.

They did well enough at the backbreaking work to attract the attention of the Yukon Mining Company, owned by Joe Ramstad, who had been mining in Flat, Alaska. Joe bought up the claims at Kako. The new owners started ground sluicing[8] half a mile north of the present retreat center. Then they brought a team to explore possibilities in Kako Creek. The team's driller was Alex Mingo.

World War II Takes Precedence

The workers began in the valley where Kako's runway lies today and mined up the creek for about 2,000 feet. By the start of World War II in 1941, they'd taken out over 4,000 ounces of gold. They called their operation the Buster Creek Mine. After the bombing of Pearl Harbor and the country's sudden plunge into WWII, Americans feared that the Japanese would attack the West Coast or far-flung American outposts in Alaska. The country needed a supply road, and needed it fast, to move personnel and equipment between the Lower 48 states and Alaska.

Government representatives visited all the working mines in Alaska. They ordered the owners to loan their machinery to build an 800-mile road through Canada. "Shut down your plants," Dave Penz quoted them, "and help us build the Alaska Highway." The companies were told that if they cooperated, they'd be given contracts to work on certain sections of the road.

Yukon Mining Company officials barged most of their machinery away from the mine to work on the 50 miles of road they were offered. They actually completed only 35 miles of the road, still an accomplishment considering the wild country and climate they dealt with. Most of the miners accompanied the equipment, but Alex Mingo stayed behind at Kako. During the war years, he worked alone, drilling to find more gold. He found it at what is known now as the Kako Mine. He filed the required government reports for the Yukon Mining Company and kept on mining.

8   See Appendix A, Methods of Ground Sluicing and Drilling for Gold, for detail on how gold was mined at and around Kako, Alaska.

Alex Mingo Carries On

When the Yukon Mining Company finished its work on the Alaska Highway, its officials decided to rename their business Ramstad Construction Company, using the name of the company's founder. They sent a letter to Alex at the Buster Creek Mine, telling him, "We're not going to pay you for any more work. We've decided to build roads instead."

Alex replied, "That's fine. I'll keep on working, but I'll record the reports in my own name." That is called top filing—the legal way to change ownership for a mine. From then on, he recorded all his work in his own name, and the mine became his. Alex continued to work mostly alone until 1957, when a young schoolteacher from Indiana, Edison Hooley, entered the picture.

Ed Hooley Comes to Kako

Ed, just out of college, had hitchhiked to Alaska and found his way to the village of Russian Mission, not far from Kako, where he accepted a job as the town's first schoolteacher. He was an energetic and likable young Christian. The village kids loved him and hung on him constantly. To get a break, he'd pick up mail for Alex at Russian Mission on Friday evenings and walk the 13-mile trail to Kako, then stay and help Alex mine until Sunday.

Ed taught four years at Russian Mission and then moved to other schools. He became a ham radio operator and also earned enough money to buy a Cessna 140 airplane. He continued to work with Alex and to help missionaries in the area.

When the Penzes came to Shageluk in June 1963, Ed came by in his plane to meet the new missionaries. The men discovered a mutual interest in ham radio. One night Ed called Dave on the radio, concerned about Alex, who was ill with what would later be diagnosed as cancer. Because Alex felt cold all the time, Ed wanted to get a warm sleeping bag to keep him comfortable at night. Dave had an Eddie Bauer catalogue and offered to order one of the best bags available. It cost around $100 back in the 1960s, but Ed Hooley gladly paid for it and wouldn't accept repayment from Alex. So Alex whipped out a piece of paper and deeded a half ownership in his mining claims to Ed.

Ed Hooley's Dream

By February 1977, the Penzes had moved to Anchorage, where they were facilitators for the needs of area missionaries with Arctic Missions Inc. The Penzes often hosted missionaries and Native guests who had business in Anchorage.

The Fur Rendezvous, an annual 10-day celebration, was in full swing that February. Dave and Janet's home overflowed with guests. Some were staff members from Victory Bible Camp who were manning a booth at the trade fair and finishing up a float for the big Fur Rondy Grand Parade. An Eskimo couple and an Indian family from outlying villages came to take part in the Native Musicale and a Christian Leadership Conference.[9] The Hooleys were also due to arrive in Anchorage shortly.

Ed Hooley had married Joyce Kauffman eight years previously. They were both teaching school at Aniak, 60 miles from Kako. By this time, Alex Mingo had died, leaving the mine to Ed, who maintained it during the summers.

Camp work was also a big part of life for the Hooleys. Ed had helped Dave that first summer at Camp Inowak. After Ed and Joyce were married, they worked with other bush camps as well and dreamed of developing a camp at Kako. Dave had pledged to help them the coming summer by lining up workers and flying in campers for at least one week of camp.

Ed and Joyce were concerned about the lack of opportunities for fellowship among Christian adults living in remote areas of the state. They were often excluded by their own people and

9   Information for the latter part of the previous chapter and this chapter comes from Janet Penz's booklet, *Where in the World Is Kako, Alaska? And What in the World Are David and Janet Penz Doing There?* (self-published, January 15, 1981).

became desperately lonely. The Hooleys looked forward to the first Kuskokwim Fellowship Conference to be held at the village of Red Devil, Alaska, the weekend of March 25–27. They had requested help from Arctic Missions Inc. to develop the conference. AMI had referred the request to Dave Penz and Greg Perry, the AMI men most acquainted with the Kuskokwim area, and Dave and Greg had met with the Hooleys in Aniak to go over plans for the conference.

Along with general activities that were part of the Rondy, the missionaries and their Native friends also had a full schedule of ministry-related activities. One was the annual board meeting for Tanalian Bible Camp.

Flying their own small plane, Ed and Joyce Hooley left their home in Aniak to attend the board meeting. On the way, they landed at Stony River to unload a passenger, and then continued on via Merrill Pass across the mountains toward Anchorage.

In the midst of all the activity at the Penz home that February 18 came an alarming phone call. Ed and Joyce were overdue on their flight plan.

Overdue

Plane overdue. The phrase strikes fear into the hearts of Alaskans. In the dead of winter, even if a pilot can land his stricken craft on a frozen lake or glacier, bad weather makes survival uncertain.

Merrill Pass is a shortcut through the Alaska Range, walled in by jagged stone peaks rising like teeth from a shark's jawbone. Over the years, treacherous weather conditions have left numerous wrecked planes scattered along the valley floor or smashed against rock walls. Now Ed and Joyce Hooley were lost somewhere in that frigid wilderness.

Those who loved them hovered near the telephone to check with flight service, while Fur Rendezvous festivities went on without them. Silently, Jan prayed, *Please, God, please let them be alive . . . Please let the weather clear . . . Help somebody to find them . . . soon.*

Dave waited too, mentally visualizing the terrain of the pass. He planned to join the search as soon as weather allowed. Finally, three days after the Hooleys disappeared, February 20 dawned clear and sunny. Dave lifted off early, flying toward Stony River, the last place they had stopped.

At the summit of Merrill Pass, he saw another small plane circling over something below. He recognized the aircraft as belonging to Dave Wilder, another friend of the Hooleys. Dave Penz began to circle also. There, just below the summit, was the Stinson 108 Ed had been flying, smashed against the rocks. He saw no sign of life. Both pilots radioed in the location of the crash.

Bad News

Immediately the area was sealed off from unofficial aircraft. A rescue helicopter set out. Late in the day, the Penzes got the sad word: "There are no survivors." The plane had hit hard, killing Ed and Joyce on impact. Both had died of broken necks. Rescuers noted a heavy buildup of ice on the leading edges of the plane's wings, along with a half-inch coating that covered the entire plane. The ice had added so much weight that the plane couldn't rise over the summit of the pass. Then, before rescuers could remove the bodies, they had to flee as another winter storm moved across the Alaska Range.

As soon as Joyce Hooley's parents, Lee and Freda Kauffman, got the news, they and Joyce's two brothers flew in from Michigan. They took care of legal matters, as well as the disposal of the couple's belongings. They planned the funeral, memorial services, and burial. Because Dave knew Aniak well and had spent time in the Hooleys' home there, he accompanied the family to help with the many decisions they needed to make. While in Aniak, he arranged and led a memorial service with the Hooleys' village friends.

It was March 3 before a memorial service for the Hooleys could be held in Anchorage. Dave led that one also. The service featured spontaneous eulogies from the congregation, in addition to a message of challenge and comfort from Chuck Crapuchettes, who knew Ed and Joyce as schoolteachers in Iliamna and had worked with them at Tanalian Bible Camp. Chuck challenged his listeners to fill in the empty spaces and carry on the Hooleys' work. In the midst of grief, the people rejoiced at two lives well lived.

The Dream Changes Hands

Before the Kauffmans returned home, they asked Dave to serve as executor for the Hooley estate. He agreed to do so.

Meanwhile, the Penzes tried to settle back into routine. Their four children attended four different schools, each with their own schedules. The two oldest, Jeanne and Valerie, had part-time jobs. Jan wrote that home "often seemed like a launching pad, with individual family members 'blasting off' into his or her separate orbit at varying times of the day or night." The family still hosted guests for the Anchorage Arctic Missions, Inc., and their home was still the purchasing and expediting center for AMI.

Less than a month later, the first Kuskokwim Fellowship Conference was held at the village of Red Devil as the Hooleys, Dave, and others had planned. This was a start toward fulfilling the needs of Christian adults, scattered in remote areas, who had little fellowship with other believers.

Then came the weeks of camping season at Camp Inowak, among the most blessed ever seen there in terms of staffing, good weather, and a cooperative spirit among the teenage campers. Everyone was grateful for the gifts of game meats, berries, and other items from Ed and Joyce's pantry. The family had also donated the Hooleys' kitchen utensils and linens.

Later in the summer, Dave caught a ride with a helicopter pilot working for a mineral survey team and flew to a spot near the summit of Merrill Pass. Alone, Dave climbed to the crash site.

Among the rocks and remaining snowbanks, he found a number of items for the family to treasure: a purse, a camera, and other personal effects. After seeing the wreckage and considering the rescue team's reports, he felt sure that ice really had been the culprit. The only good option for a pilot encountering icing is to descend to lower altitude. Perhaps Ed was so close to crossing the pass he chose the risk of continuing on rather than the risk of trying to turn around and go back.

CHAPTER 13
Gold Mine to Bible Camp? Is It Possible?

Just a few weeks prior to the accident, when Dave had met with the Hooleys in Aniak, they had discussed their hopes of turning Ed's gold mine at Kako into a Bible camp, which would also provide a place for adult retreats and conferences. Later, Dave shared the conversation with the families. The families of both Ed and Joyce wished to give the mine to Arctic Missions, Inc., for development as a camp. However, when Dave began looking into the possibility, the project turned out to be much more complicated than it first appeared.

Although the Hooleys owned the rights to mine ore in the ground at Kako, they didn't actually own the land. To keep the mining rights, they or their heirs had only to make yearly improvements and record the improvements with the proper office. But to put a camp there required having title to the land itself.

Three steps were involved in getting title, and each had to be scheduled with and approved by the US government. First, AMI would have to arrange and pay for a survey of the ground, with officially approved surveyors. That cost about $7,000 in 1977 dollars. Second, US mineralogists had to do a mineral survey of each claim to be sure there was sufficient ore for profitable mining. Last, if the mineral survey were approved, AMI would have to purchase the land from the government, which at that time cost $2.50 an acre. Until all these things were accomplished, the land could be used only for mining.

In August, Joyce's father, Lee Kauffman, returned from Michigan to help Dave with the necessary assessment work at the mine. They cleared brush and labored to widen the airstrip. More than ever, Dave imagined a camp and retreat center there. Again, he asked Arctic Missions, Inc. to consider the possibility of such a project. AMI asked him to write up a full report.

Later in August, Dave and the family left Anchorage for a five-month furlough in the Lower 48. They intended to represent AMI in meetings in Virginia and Tennessee and visit supporters and churches to share their work with them. They also planned to spend time with friends and relatives in the Midwest.

In their travels, they stopped in Goshen, Indiana, to meet Ed Hooley's sister, Ella Mae, and their elderly mother. The women played a tape for the Penzes that Ed and Joyce had recorded and sent to them just before the accident. On it they sang, "What a Day That Will Be," a gospel song popular at that time. As Jan listened to the dear familiar voices singing about heaven and the wonder of seeing face to face he who saves us by his grace, she remembered when the Hooleys had sent her a request to find the song's lyrics and music and mail them to Aniak. It had seemed like only another routine request, part of Jan's job. Now, she wrote, it was "another reminder that we just have no way of knowing the future or the impact our seemingly unimportant tasks may have on the lives of others."

Roadblocks

Back in their home state of Minnesota, the Penzes typed up a report to send to AMI's Alaska Field Council. They listed reasons why Kako Mine would be an excellent place to develop a Bible camp and named all the villages in the area, over 50 of them within a radius of 160 miles. Many had no access at all to the Good News of Jesus Christ.

The Field Council's reply thanked the Penzes for the good report and for drawing attention to the needs of the area. AMI did hope to place some missionaries there soon, but they didn't have the resources to develop the mine into a camp. There was also another conflict. AMI needed to remain a nonprofit organization, but in order to establish ownership of the land, the mine had to operate at a profit for a certain period of time.

A few days later, Dave and Jan received a letter from Ella Mae Hooley. She had just been contacted by the former owner of the mine, the man who had abandoned it to Alex Mingo years before. This man had earlier offered to pay her brother $500 for the mining rights, but Ed had turned the offer down. Now the former owner accused Ed of taking some items from the mine that that man had previously abandoned when he'd left Kako. He demanded payment from the family for some welding rods and the cost of recovering other equipment. They all felt grieved and outraged that Ed Hooley's good name should be smeared when he was not there to defend himself.

After they'd returned to Alaska, Dave had stopped to check on the mine at Kako and found signs posted: "No Trespassing. Property of Mr. X and Sons." Of course, it was not Mr. X's property but the government's, so Dave took the signs down.

As representative of the Hooley estate, Dave was served in July with a court summons to answer the charge that the estate owed Mr. X for some things "stolen" from "his" mine. A hearing was scheduled for December.

During the intervening time, Dave spent hours learning all he could about transactions having to do with Kako. He paged through volumes of old records at the Alaska Department of Natural Resources' District Recorder's Office and made copies of pertinent documents for the judge, who finally settled the case in favor of the Hooley estate.

With that problem out of the way, Dave began to look for a buyer for the mining rights—someone who would work the mine and patent the ground,[10] and when the mining was finished, give the land back to him so a camp could be established. Several people were interested but couldn't commit to working toward ownership of the land. One Christian businessman had contributed to the Penzes' support over the years and had paid for special mission projects when he saw a real need. But Dave couldn't ensure that the mine would be a profitable investment, nor could he ensure that the ground could be patented or a camp established. It was a big request, a "far out" idea, but he couldn't give it up.

Meanwhile, the Penzes continued with their usual busy schedule, which included planning for conferences, Camp Inowak's children's and family camps, and a ladies' retreat. Dave again was elected to serve on the mission field council.

The Need Becomes Clearer

When the council met in September 1979, a person representing one of the Yukon River villages brought a request. Could the council provide a quiet place away from the village where couples and families could go for fellowship and study? Council members discussed the request and decided to try to schedule something at Victory Bible Camp.

Dave liked the idea, but he could see potential difficulties. Victory Bible Camp was in the mountains, a long way from the Yukon River. Getting people there would be difficult. Cultural values of indigenous people-groups differed, too. It would be better to have this quiet place nearer the homes of the people he ministered to. Kako was close to the mouth of the Yukon in Southwestern Alaska. The people in that area were mostly Yupik,

---

10 A patented mining claim is one for which the federal government has passed its title to the claimant, making it private land. A person may mine and remove minerals from a mining claim without a mineral patent. However, a mineral patent gives the owner exclusive title to the locatable minerals. It also gives the owner title to the surface and other resources. Per the "Mining Claims" page on the website for 1881.com Investments: http://www.1881.com/minedef.htm. Accessed June 5, 2018.

as opposed to the mostly Athabaskan people near Victory Bible Camp.[11] Kako already had an airstrip, some buildings, and plenty of room to expand. It could be transformed into a year-round retreat center where people could come for onsite seminars, counseling, and encouragement. It would be a place for asking questions and learning in a homey, relaxing atmosphere. Children and teens could attend camp in the summer. But who would be willing to manage all this? And who would be willing to invest financially?

---

11   The Alaska Native Heritage Center explains that Native Alaskan people belong to 11 distinct cultures, speaking 11 different languages and 22 different dialects.

Athabascan: The Athabascan people traditionally lived in Interior Alaska along five major river systems: the Yukon, the Tanana, the Susitna, the Kuskokwim, and the Copper River. (Athabascan Cultures of Alaska, accessed March 19, 2015, http://www.alaskanative.net/en/main-nav/education-and-programs/cultures-of-alaska/athabascan.)

Unangax and *Alutiiq (Sugpiak)*: These are maritime people living in South and Southwest Alaska, all the way from Prince William Sound through the Aleutian Island chain. Russian colonizers gave them the name Aleuts. (Unangax & Alutiiq [Sugpiaq] Cultures of Alaska, accessed March 19, 2015, http://www.alaskanative.net/en/main-nav/education-and-programs/cultures-of-alaska/unangax-and-alutiiq.)

Yup'ik and *Cup'ik*: These Southwest Alaska Natives are named after the two main dialects of the Yupik language. Most of the people within the range of Kako's influence are Yup'ik. (Yup'ik and Cup'ik Cultures of Alaska, accessed March 19, 2015, http://www.alaskanative.net/en/main-nav/education-and-programs/cultures-of-alaska/yupik-and-cupik.)

Inupiaq and *St. Lawrence Island Yupik*: Calling themselves the "Real People," these groups continue to subsist on the land and sea of North and Northwest Alaska. (Inupiaq & St. Lawrence Island Yupik Cultures of Alaska, accessed March 19, 2015, http://www.alaskanative.net/en/main-nav/education-and-programs/cultures-of-alaska/inupiaq-and-stlawrence-island.)

Eyak, Tlingit, Haida and *Timshian*: These four groups are neighbors, occupying the Pacific Northwest Coast from the Copper River Delta to the Southeast panhandle. They share a common and similar culture, with important differences in language and clan system. (Eyak, Tlingit, Haida and Tsimshian Cultures of Alaska, accessed March 19, 2015, http://www.alaskanative.net/en/main-nav/education-and-programs/cultures-of-alaska/eyak-tlingit-haida-and-tsimshian.)

New Directions

Dave contacted the Christian businessman again, explaining that the price of gold had climbed to a record high. That made the investment more attractive. The businessman replied: "I'll invest only if you will take charge of the mining operation."

Now Dave was on the spot. If he did the mining, he and Jan would have to take a leave of absence from the mission, for which they'd worked 18 years. They'd have to turn Camp Inowak and other ministries over to someone else. Were they willing to do that? Dave thought about the possibility of working several years to earn the land, only to fail to find enough gold to make it pay. He also knew the price of gold could drop again.

He weighed the pros and cons. If the project were to work out, it needed a leader who held a vision of what a camp could mean to the area. It needed someone who cared enough to put everything he had into making it a success. That someone should be familiar with heavy equipment and earthmoving operations. He also should be someone who was experienced in camping and conference work, someone who really cared for the Native people and knew how to work alongside them and who cared about their cultural values. He should know the area, preferably as a pilot, and should enjoy hard work.

Dave was startled to realize that he himself fit all those requirements.

Then in November, he took a couple of leaders of New Life Native Fellowship to Minneapolis to attend a seminar on Christian principles. For a week, the classes built one principle upon another. Special materials had recently been produced, locking these principles into culturally appropriate illustrations and teachings. The Native leaders found the teachings invaluable. What if these kinds of seminars could be held at Kako?

The following month, Dave took a trip to several Kuskokwim-Yukon villages. He talked with Native believers about the need for such training. They enthusiastically supported the idea.

I'll Do It

Dave still wasn't sure if buying land at Kako was just something *he* wanted to do, or if it was truly the Lord's leading in his life. So he discussed it with the pastors of their Anchorage church. The three men prayed about it. Then with relief and a sense of freedom, Dave announced, "I'll do it."

He and Jan applied for leaves of absence from AMI. One day, an engineer who had earlier worked for the Hooley estate, called to tell Dave he'd discovered a reference to Kako Mine in an old government document. The document mentioned that a team from the University of Alaska had been at Kako in the summer of 1940 and had tested for ore.

Dave searched in vain for information at the Federal Resource Library in Anchorage. When he asked the librarian if other resource material was available, she suggested checking with the University of Alaska's Geology Department in Fairbanks. Dave called and stated his question to the professor who answered the telephone. The professor said, "Sure. I was a student on that trip. What do you want to know?"

The professor found records of the testing done 40 years earlier. The records stated that some ore was on the claims, but it was buried deep underground. The overburden would have to be stripped away before mining could take place. An efficient operation would be needed to make mining profitable.

That same day, Dave called another government office to establish permission to travel the six miles between the mine site and the Yukon River. The official said he had just put that file away and that Dave already had the easement rights.

When the estate's lawyer and the families heard the new information, the lawyer wanted to spend more time and money investigating in hopes of selling at a higher price. But the Hooleys and the Kauffmans wanted to see Ed and Joyce's dream carried forward. They favored selling to the Christian businessman at the already agreed-upon price. So each heir signed off on the claims, and in late August the mining rights were officially sold. It was three and a half years after the accident, and three months after the Penzes' leave of absence had begun.

Dave and Jan stood poised on the edge of a new work. They longed to see the dream become reality. They also knew that if Kako Retreat Center was to be established, they must depend on the prayers of God's people. It was a time of excitement, challenge, and complete trust in God's leading.

In 1980, the Penzes' businessman friend who'd bought the mining rights hauled mining equipment to Kako. After working for two years, he'd taken out a good amount of gold and made over a half million dollars. Then the price of gold dropped, as did his profits. He ceased mining and waited a year to see if the price would rise again. It didn't, and he decided to sell his rights. Dave offered to buy them, but the man said, "How can you? You have no money."

Dave and Jan discussed it. Years before, while recuperating from lung surgery at the Mayo Clinic in Minnesota, Dave had learned that the clinic had a long-range expansion plan. He bought an old house nearby, knowing that in about 10 years the clinic would have to purchase and demolish such properties to expand. He remodeled the house into apartments and kept them rented. The income from those properties had helped support the family all this time. Perhaps they could pay off the businessman and take over the mining themselves if they gave up their land and apartments in Minnesota.

The properties were appraised at $250,000, a large amount in the early 1980s, but the businessman wanted more. However, the price of gold stayed down, and he had no other offers. He tried to pull his machinery to the river so he could barge it out, but since there was no road yet, it got stuck in mud. Finally he agreed to Dave's offer.

During this time, Dave and their 12-year-old son, Jonathan, spent time at the mine doing the required caretaking and assessment work, which included building and maintaining access roads and an airstrip, constructing buildings that benefited the claim, and drilling and sampling the soil. In this way the Penzes learned where the gold was and what they needed to do.

Beginning a New Phase

After the businessman agreed to sell, Dave took over the mining rights and equipment. So, three and a half years following the plane crash that ended Ed and Joyce Hooley's involvement in the Kako dream, the Penzes began to transform a gold mine into a center that would bring imperishable riches to Alaska's Yukon-Kuskokwim people.

The family moved to Kako and lived there year-round in an old mining building. By this time, daughter Jeanne had met John Rodkey at Multnomah School of the Bible and had married him. (Originally from Eastern Washington, John had volunteered at Camp Inowak as a way to get to know Jeanne and her world better. It worked.) The other girls also went away to school, and Jan home-schooled Jonathan. With the help of another man, Dave and Jonathan continued mining together. The price of gold rose a little, and they made enough money to live on, though not enough to support a retreat center. But they never lost sight of their dream for a ministry center. They continued their friendships with people from the villages and did what they could to share the Good News of the gospel.

Boldness + Creativity = Solution

When Dave needed a Caterpillar for construction projects, his boldness created a solution.

At the close of World War II, the US government shipped surplus Caterpillar D7s from Tokyo and gave them to villages in Alaska. Many machines ended up unusable because no one took responsibility for their maintenance. One day, Dave happened to see one of these D7s abandoned in brush at Russian Mission. He looked it over and saw that the block was cracked. No one had drained the engine before winter, and when the water froze and expanded, it cracked the block.

Dave asked if he could have the useless piece of equipment. Village authorities shrugged and said "yes" to the crazy white man. He bought another block, exchanged parts and tuned up the machine.

Early one morning the Cat roared to life and woke up the whole village. Dave drove the bulldozer out of the brush to where the barge was tied up, loaded it, and had it barged upriver to Kako Landing. Some villagers were put out, thinking that Dave ought to pay them for the machine. So he gave them $250.

He used the Caterpillar a lot on the road that ran from Kako Landing to the end of the airstrip. He would scoop out ditches on either side of the road, pile the dirt in the center, and then grade it level. That created a drivable winter roadbed once the ground froze. He also used the Cat to haul heavy items, such as diesel fuel and aviation gas, from river barges. Additional uses were keeping the airstrip itself in shape, moving dirt at the mine, and dragging logs to the sawmill.

Tragedy for the Penz Family

Tragedy struck in 1986, after the family had been at Kako for six years. The situation began when Jan went into early menopause. Her body ran low on estrogen, and the resulting chemical imbalance threw her into depression again. Dave took her to a doctor who prescribed lithium-based antidepressants. They worked, but Jan felt intense guilt over her inability to live a victorious Christian life without the aid of medication.

As she battled intensifying symptoms, trying to adapt, the cold, dark days of winter seemed to echo her own feelings of hopelessness and being trapped. In the midst of her extreme mental and emotional pain, beautiful, vivacious Jan ended her own life. She was only 49. She and Dave had been married for 31 years.

Her death devastated the family. Each member struggled to carry on without her. With great sorrow, they gathered to bury her at Palmer, Alaska. Then the girls went back to their individual lives, still trying to make sense of what had happened, and Dave and Jonathan returned to a bleak Kako.

CHAPTER 14
Vera

Needed: a Wife

Dave and Jonathan continued their lonely work at the mine. But what would become of the Kako dream now? Dave couldn't mine and run a retreat center at the same time, especially after adding in the business part of it, plus the cooking, cleaning, and meeting other challenges of life in the Alaskan bush. As time went on and the shock and grief of losing Jan eased a little, Dave realized that as a matter of practicality, he needed someone to stand beside him and help carry the load. He needed a wife.

This woman would have to share his love for Native peoples and be experienced in working with them. She must be fearless in facing wilderness life and unfazed by the lack of civilized amenities. She couldn't be afraid of flying or river travel. She needed to be strong and healthy, a hard worker. The list was long.

Dave set out to find someone who fit his specifications.

Of course he prayed about the matter—a lot. And he felt God give him an idea. He would make a tape recording telling about himself and his dreams for Kako and send or give it to women who might be candidates.

Some Native girls set their caps for the good-looking missionary. He noticed them when he flew to Russian Mission to get the mail. They'd dress up and wait for him with alluring smiles in the post office. Single ladies with ministries of their own wrote to suggest that perhaps Dave would like to join them in California or wherever their work happened to be. A year went by, and he felt he'd reached a dead end. Was he supposed to abandon his dream for Kako?

Then he attended a missions conference at Victory Bible Camp. At one of the meals, Dave sat next to an acquaintance, Vera Kelley. He had known about her for years. He'd heard of the death of her husband Al, her continuing ministry at Glennallen, and then of her move to Fairbanks 15 years earlier. In turn, Vera had heard of Jan's death through mutual missionary acquaintances and had been praying for Dave. The two of them spent time catching up.

The following day, Vera attended an early morning prayer meeting. One request was for Dave Penz, who needed a wife if he was to carry on with the vision God had given him for Kako. So Vera prayed along with the others that God would give Dave a wife. It never occurred to her that since she'd loved and worked with Alaska's Native people for many years, both in the bush and in the city, and she had bookkeeping and organizational skills, she could be invaluable to an undertaking like Kako.

But these things didn't escape Dave's notice. He saw in small, silver-haired Vera, who glowed with good health and the love of the Lord, a woman who'd put God first in her life in spite of the pain of losing her husband and son. She obviously loved the people she worked with. Might she be the wife Dave was asking for?

The conference ended, and they both went back to work— Vera in Fairbanks and Dave at Kako. Dave wanted to get better acquainted, but he needed an excuse to call her. Then he thought of a man he knew who was in prison in Fairbanks.

An Unorthodox Courtship

Dave dialed Vera's number, and the call went through. She answered, and he stammered a bit as he gave her the story of the man in prison.

That's funny, Vera thought. *Usually men reach out to the men. Why is he calling me?*

She said as much, and Dave took a deep breath and came out with his real reason for calling. "I need to be married," he said. "I'm seeking God's will for my life, and he brought you to mind. Would you be interested in getting to know me better?"

Vera's mind whirled. Other men had paid attention to her, but she'd felt no answering interest. Her busy ministry in Fairbanks occupied most of her time. She was content living as a single person. She explained that to Dave, then added, "I haven't shut the door to remarriage. But the Lord would have to make it clear that this is what he wants for me."

Dave's heart leaped. She hadn't said no. "I'd like to send you a tape to tell you about myself and my family," he said.

After Vera agreed that he could send it, they hung up. She felt excited about the call but uncertain too. It would be a big step for her to continue the friendship. It was true that she was content and busy, but at 53 years of age, she dealt with occasional pangs of loneliness. Like anyone in her situation, she felt a little scared of growing old alone.

She thought back to one time when she'd given of herself in service to needy people until her energies were drained. Longing to get away to relax for a while, she'd thought of a couple who were close friends. She called them. They'd invited her to come to their home outside of town for an evening of games and relaxation. It helped, but not enough. Driving home that cold, starry winter night, Vera had prayed, "God, I just need to have a special awareness of who you are. Please, I need a new touch from you." She turned the radio on, and as she drove up over a hill, a panorama of snow-covered forest rolled out before her, overhung with a breathtaking and colorful display of the aurora borealis. As curtains of light swirled across the sky, a song came over the radio, "Come into His Presence Singing Alleluia." Vera felt that God met her there on that hilltop with encouragement tailored just for her.

On other occasions when she'd felt discouraged, God brought people into her life to encourage her. Sometimes she would hear of someone who had come to know Jesus through her ministry or through hearing the story of Al's death. God thus encouraged her to keep working and trusting him.

Although she was excited about Dave's call, she also knew it would be a huge step of faith for her to continue the friendship. When Dave sent the tape, she listened to it, but as she listened, she told herself, *I don't have time to get to know this man. There he is, way out at Kako, and I'm so involved with my work here in Fairbanks.* Encouraging Dave might mean she would have to leave her ministry to go to Kako. She wasn't ready for that. She didn't know how to tell Dave no, and she wasn't ready to say yes, so she put the tape way and never acknowledged receiving it.

One day while she was leading a Bible study for Native women in her Fairbanks home, the phone rang. One of the women answered the phone. After the study, she told Vera, "It was a man named Dave Penz. He wanted to know if you ever got a tape he sent."

Vera felt a twinge of guilt, but she still did nothing about it. She'd listened to it but hadn't really "tuned in" to it.

A year went by, and Dave became discouraged. He felt like the prophet Samuel who had gone to Jesse's house because God had told him to anoint the king God had chosen. Jesse brought in many sons as possible candidates, but the one Samuel looked for was missing.

Thinking of how Jesse had finally brought in his last son from the fields where he shepherded his father's flocks—David, Israel's future king—Dave said to God, "I give up. You're going to have to find the wife you want for me."

Meanwhile during that year, Dave's name came before Vera at random times and in different conversations. People would mention what a fine person he was and how he loved the Native people.

Then she had an opportunity to revisit Tatitlek, where she and Al had ministered 30 years before. She rode with the Olsons, a couple from Cordova who were now flying weekly to Tatitlek to lead Bible study and services. From the air, they pointed out

Johnson Cove, the place where the *Evangel* had capsized. Once in the village, Vera recognized familiar faces of children they had ministered to, now grown up. She was warmly received in the homes, visiting and renewing acquaintances.

Mrs. Olson had been one of the Tatitlek children who'd trusted in the Lord. Because of strong opposition by the Russian Orthodox Church to any of their people listening to Protestants, the young woman had moved to Cordova. She married there. Then she and her husband came back to Tatitlek. Because they owned property in the village, they could not be put out. They established a church. Vera was thrilled to find other former Sunday school students now walking with the Lord. In fact, one third of the villagers were now believers. Many still attended the Orthodox church, but when they needed someone to help them, they went to Protestant believers.

While in Tatitlek, Vera stayed in the home of a Native family whose mother, Ann Jackson, told her about her son in Anchorage who had come to faith in the Lord through the witness of a remarkable man named David Penz.

God Gives Vera a Push

Once she was home again in Fairbanks, more time went by. At two o'clock one early morning in October, Vera woke from peaceful sleep with Dave on her mind. Had he been in a plane crash? Was he in some other kind of trouble? Vera was quite sure the Lord had awakened her. She prayed fervently for Dave and then lay down again, but she couldn't sleep.

So she got up, found the tape, and listened to it again. It seemed that she was actually hearing it for the first time. As she listened to Dave's voice, she heard a man who loved the Lord above all, who loved the Native people, and to whom God had given a vision. That vision was to reach out to people in the isolated villages of Western Alaska and to make a safe place for them to rest, learn, and grow. In spite of opposition and the heartache of losing his wife, he'd persevered and kept his eyes on the Lord and the vision God had given him.

Vera felt amazed. *We do have a lot in common,* she thought. *I do want to get to know him better.* God had used that intervening year to prepare her heart for a new adventure.

She sat down and wrote Dave a letter. "A year has passed," she said, "and you could be married now, but if not, I *am* interested in getting to know you better."

CHAPTER 15
New Joy

While Vera composed her letter to him, Dave continued his work at Kako, still praying but feeling disheartened. The tasks were overwhelming for a person alone, and his dreams for Kako seemed out of reach. Although he would never wish Jan back to suffer as she'd done in her final months, the Alaskan wilderness seemed lonely, especially with another long, cold winter coming on. None of his friendships with potential partners had worked out. Even Vera, the perfect candidate as far as he was concerned, the woman to whom he already hoped to entrust his heart, did not seem interested in him or in Kako.

"Lord, I don't know where to turn next," he prayed.

Then the mail plane brought Vera's letter.

Getting to Know Each Other

When Dave read Vera's message, his heart somersaulted with joy. His legs got so weak he had to sit down. Vera wanted to get to know him better!

Before he could lose his courage, he got ready for a snow machine ride to Russian Mission and the nearest telephone. He drove into town and stopped beside the town telephone, fastened to the outside wall of a shed. Standing there while villagers roared by on their snow machines, he dialed her number, then waited impatiently for her to pick up the receiver.

Vera answered. Trying hard to suppress her own excitement at the sound of Dave's voice, she made small talk for a few moments. Then Dave said, "I got your letter. Would you like to come to Kako?"

"Ummm . . . why don't you come to Fairbanks?"

So they made a date, and Dave flew to Fairbanks. They tried to appear casual about the meeting, because Vera wished to attract as little attention as possible. With many people coming and going in her home and with all those with whom she shared her life and ministry, she often felt like she lived in a fishbowl. People watched her, and if they suspected anything out of the ordinary about her visit with Dave, there'd certainly be more questions than she wanted to answer. She confided in only one coworker, her friend Lynne Hounsell.

Early on a Sunday morning, Dave flew five hours from Kako to Fairbanks International Airport. Vera watched as his plane touched down. Later, she said when she saw the tall, muscular man descend from the plane to the tarmac, "My heart flipped!" She drove him to a restaurant where they ate breakfast and talked for hours. Because they had so many experiences in common and knew so many of the same people, they felt as if they'd been friends for years.

Friends or mission coworkers often came to Fairbanks. It was not uncommon for Vera to provide transportation for them, even single men, showing them around and taking them to church. That morning she took Dave to her Baptist church. Only one woman thought it was unusual enough to ask them what was going on. Dave answered, "I'm just in town for the day. Vera is my chauffeur."

Later that day they visited the Fairbanks Native Bible Church, where Vera regularly played piano. Dave already knew Mark Anaruk, who was leading the singing. (Mark had played the guitar as a 15-year-old at Camp Inowak.) Mark asked Dave to tell the group about Kako. With new enthusiasm, Dave shared his vision of a retreat center for the Yukon-Kuskokwim Delta Native people. After that, Dave took Vera to dinner at a nice restaurant, and then he returned to Kako.

Letters flew back and forth between Kako and Fairbanks until Christmastime, when each of them flew to the Lower 48—Dave to visit his daughter Jeanne and family, and Vera to spend the holiday with daughter Debbie and family. When Dave called Vera at Debbie's home, Deb knew something special was in the air.

Vera Meets Kako

By this time both Dave and Vera felt that God was bringing them together. However, Dave knew Vera needed to visit Kako to see if she could live there. So in January, after they'd both returned to Alaska, Vera caught a flight to Galena. Dave picked her up there in his Cessna 180. It was 30 degrees below zero as they swooped between the hills onto Kako's snow-covered airstrip. Vera saw nothing but trees and a few tiny mining cabins. Dave's daughter Valerie ran from one of the cabins to welcome them. Father and daughter were the only people staying there at the time.

Valerie had prepared one of the cabins for Vera to stay in. She did the cooking for them so Dave and Vera could spend a lot of time just talking and getting to know one another.

Dave gave Vera the list of the expectations he had for a wife.

"Are you sure you don't want to inspect my teeth?" she joked. But she had her own list for a prospective husband. It didn't take long for each to decide that the other measured up.

One day they rode Dave's snow machine to the top of the nearby mountain so Vera could see the expanse of rolling hills and the frozen Yukon in the distance. The landscape was vast and awe-inspiring. Dave pointed out where some of more than 50 villages lay within the 160-mile radius that Kako would serve. As he told her of the changes he hoped the gospel would bring to those villages, Vera felt her own heart lift to embrace those people who so sorely needed Jesus.

Another day they flew to Marshall, about 20 air miles west of Kako, to visit in the home of a Native couple there. The woman gave Dave a big hug and said with tears, "I'm so glad you came. I was praying that someone would come." She'd just returned from her brother's funeral. The two visitors read Scripture, prayed, and sang gospel songs with the woman. Then she fed them a snack of homemade white bread and canned eels. The eels were a first for Vera.

They snow-machined to Russian Mission to pick up the mail and visit Dave's friends there. Vera felt comfortable working alongside the big missionary. Before she returned to Fairbanks, she and Dave each promised to write and let the other know how he or she felt the Lord directing.

But Vera was already quite sure that God was leading the two of them together and that he was giving her a love for Dave. Home again, she wrote a letter telling Dave this.

The Course of True Love Never Runs Smooth

Vera waited for his reply to come, but she received nothing. "Oh, no," she thought. "He's changed his mind." She found out later that after Dave had left her in Galena where she caught a larger plane to Fairbanks, he had to land and stay in some of the villages for days because of bad weather. When the skies cleared enough for him to fly home to Kako, he wrote a letter. He put it in the mailbag in a sled that he pulled behind the snow machine, and took it over to Russian Mission to mail. He didn't realize he'd lost the sled with the mailbag in it somewhere along the way. He had to go back and look for it. So it took quite a lot longer for that letter to get to Vera than she'd expected, but it finally did arrive—on Valentine's Day. In it, Dave told her that he loved her and wanted to marry her.

Another envelope from Dave came in the same mail. It contained a beautiful leaf-shaped gold nugget, an inch long by 3/8-inch wide, mined at Kako. Though she tried to keep her feet planted firmly on the ground, Vera felt that she was floating among the clouds.

The two didn't have to wait long for the next opportunity to be together. The annual Fur Rendezvous, coming up in late February, included activities sponsored by the Anchorage Native New Life church for Native believers from all over the state. Christians came together during the Native Musicale for fellowship and to share their culture. Vera had been invited to talk to the women, and Dave would speak at a potluck for the whole group.

Both Dave and Vera had worked with the church in Anchorage for years. Now they found time to get together for more visiting. During one visit, while sitting in a downtown parking lot, Dave asked Vera if she would marry him. She said, "Yes." He wanted to go to a nearby jewelry store and find a ring immediately.

But Vera hesitated. "I can't get engaged, not yet. I have to have SEND North's permission."

"Are you serious?" Dave asked.

"Yes, I am," Vera replied. "It's in our handbook. A single person must get permission from the mission to marry if we want to stay with them. It's because who I marry will affect my ministry and my testimony. I agreed to that when I joined."

That made sense to Dave. "They'll agree—they have to agree," he said. "This is God's doing. Can't we at least look at rings?"

So they went to a jewelry store and asked to look at engagement rings. They found one that suited Vera perfectly and had it sized to fit her. Dave paid for it and gave it to Vera. "I can't put it on," she said. "Let me be sure the mission agrees, first." So he put it in his pocket, and the two of them went back to their responsibilities at the Native Musicale.

Yes!

In Anchorage they visited mutual friends, Don and Lorraine Stump. The Stumps loved Dave, and they loved Vera, and when the two told them of their plans, the Anchorage friends were overjoyed. They'd never thought of Dave and Vera together, but, they said, "We can't think of a better match." Then they told Vera that of all their missionary friends, Dave was the one who really loved the Native people. To Vera, that was a seal of sorts on their plans.

Later, back in Fairbanks, Vera called her mission director, Leander Rempel. She told him that Dave had asked her to marry him and that they wanted to be engaged. The director was so stunned he said nothing for a moment. Then he said with joy, "Vera, you have really made my day!" She had been contentedly single for over 30 years. The whole thing came as a complete surprise. But the director was delighted for her and gladly gave his permission.

While Dave and Vera were still in Anchorage, they discussed the wedding date. Because Dave would be mining all summer, it seemed wise to plan an autumn wedding. He thought getting married earlier would make Vera's adjustment difficult, with Kako's primitive conditions and with all the work that mining entailed.

But as they later talked on the phone, Vera said, "You know I've always been up to a challenge."

Dave agreed.

"Why are we waiting?" she asked.

Dave later told Debbie that one of the guys at the mine told him he might as well go and see Vera, because in his current state of mind, he was worthless for working at the mine.

They kept moving the date up and finally settled on May 14, 1988.

The Wedding

The wedding was held in Fairbanks, in a church packed with friends of Dave's and Vera's from both their missions. Don Stump from Anchorage and Vera's brother Jim Johnson from Glennallen were the pastors who performed the ceremony. Frank Severn, the director of SEND International, offered the prayer. Dwayne King of SEND—Vera's missionary friend and a good friend of Dave's as well—was Dave's best man. George Richardson and Fritz Geffe of the Native Bible Church in Fairbanks were ushers.

Vera's six-year-old granddaughter, Mandy, told her family, "I think my grandma is going to want me to be in her wedding." She was right. She got to be her grandma's flower girl. Mandy's mother, Deb, was Vera's maid of honor.

Among the guests was Vera's twin sister Connie. She had dedicated herself to caring for their mother, who lived to be 94 years of age. Also in attendance were Vera and Connie's brother Jim and his family, as well as Dave's daughters, Jeanne and Valerie. Dave's parents, both in their 80s, had come all the way from Minnesota.

As the ceremony concluded, all the guests stood and sang "My Tribute" by Andraé Crouch, giving glory to God and expressing thanks for all the things the Lord had done. As the bride and groom joined with the soaring voices of their friends, they knew their wedding had brought glory to their heavenly Father—a fitting confirmation of the merging of their two missions and a prelude to what God was going to do through them at Kako.

Following the wedding, the happy couple drove to McKinley Park, where they stayed in a rustic cabin for their wedding night. They went on to Anchorage, where a second reception was held for friends who'd not been able to come to Fairbanks for the wedding. Vera wore her wedding dress again for that special celebration. They flew from Anchorage to Maui, Hawaii, for their honeymoon, where they relaxed in the sun and talked about what the future might hold for them and the Native peoples they loved to serve.

A Wonderful Wedding Gift

They then returned to Kako. One of the first things they did was check for mail that awaited them. In the stack, they found an envelope that would determine the course of the rest of their lives. It held the patent for 80 acres of land at the mine, in a strip one mile long and an eighth of a mile wide. Kako was officially theirs! They immediately applied for nonprofit organization status with the Internal Revenue Service and for incorporation with the State of Alaska. It was May 1988. Kako Retreat Center, Inc. would soon be a legal entity.

CHAPTER 16
A Year of Firsts

Wilbert Nicholas, Dave's friend from Grayling, had spent the winter at Kako, handling emergencies whenever Dave had to be away and keeping fires burning in the old mining cabins to protect them from freezing temperatures. Dave's artist daughter Dianne wrote in the Kako newsletter—which she hand printed and illustrated—that Wilbert did a lot of trapping while he was there. "Those beavers had better watch out, or they'll wind up in his pot of stew," she teased.

After the May wedding, Vera enjoyed settling into her new home with Dave in one of the 55-year-old mine buildings beside the airstrip. The cabins were painted green with white trim. Their house, bigger than the other cabins and once the home of the mine boss, had been refurbished with large windows. Dianne and her brother Jonathan, fresh from his first year at Moody Bible Institute and a session at the Institute's flight camp, returned to spend another summer mining. Daughter Valerie, who had spent a month helping her dad at the mine, took a job in Anchorage.

Kako Retreat Center Is Official

In June, one month after Vera's arrival, Kako Retreat Center officially became a nonprofit corporation in the State of Alaska, with its articles and bylaws drawn up by an attorney. The Internal Revenue Service was processing their tax-exempt status application. Dave had already gathered a group of Alaskan men to serve Kako

Retreat Center as board members to whom he and Vera would be accountable, and on June first, he flew to Anchorage for the first official board meeting. The board discussed Kako's 80 acres of land which lay, surrounded by Native corporation land, in a valley that opened out to the Yukon River.

As was true in other parts of Alaska, the surrounding villages, populated mostly by Yupik Eskimos and a smaller number of Athabascan Indians, had long been nominally Russian Orthodox or Catholic. Sharing Dave's vision that Kako would become a place where people of all ages could receive education, counseling, encouragement, and Christian fellowship, Vera enthusiastically entered into Kako's activities.

Although she knew she was not leaving her ministry to Native people, just changing the location, she still found it difficult to resign from SEND and sever the bonds of 34 years. She wrote to those who had faithfully upheld her through prayer and financial support, some of whom had been partners from the time she and Al Kelley left New York.

She explained about the Hooleys' vision and that Dave had retired from InterAct in order to begin a new ministry at Kako to carry on their vision. She explained she was leaving SEND in order to join Dave in the new ministry. "In the past years, the land has been cleared, an airstrip made, and cabins renovated," she wrote. "This year we will be using these cabins for our retreats. We have an old sawmill that has been rebuilt, and our plan is to build more cabins and eventually a lodge."

Mining

During the short summer months, everyone's lives revolved around mining for income to support the staff, as well as to establish the retreat center.

The Environmental Protection Agency had added new rules for miners, so Dave hired a young couple and several other people to help set up a different method of gold recovery. They opened

a 40-foot-deep pit and dug drainage and settling ponds. They
built a state-of-the-art recovery plant that had new equipment and
the latest technology. It included a closed recycling system that
was more efficient and used much less water. The group actually
accomplished two seasons of work during that one season, but
unfortunately, by the time the plant was operational, freeze-up
came and stopped progress. No income would come from the mine
that year. But they trusted the Lord to meet their needs. Some
of their previous supporters continued to send gifts. Others heard
about Kako for the first time and sent contributions.

Concentrating on the Ministry

Never one to wait until funds were in hand to make plans for
the next steps, Dave worked on setting up the sawmill to make
lumber for their own building projects.

Meanwhile, once Kako Mine shut down for the season, the
Penzes were free to concentrate on the two main aspects of their
ministry: the itinerant part, where they traveled to the people;
and the retreat center, where people could come for fellowship,
teaching, and counseling.

Within the reach of their airplane, more than 50 villages needed
someone to tell them of God's love. During the preceding years,
Dave had made friends and gained the respect of people in many of
these villages. The closest village, Russian Mission, was only eight
air miles from Kako, but it took about 13 miles of driving by snow
machine to reach the village bank or post office. After the spring
thaw, they flew their plane to Russian Mission to get supplies,
mail, or to use a telephone. Dave and Vera enjoyed flying together
to other villages to visit and encourage people.

During Kako's first retreat, held Thanksgiving 1988, two
Native families—the Mark Anaruk family from Akiak, and Alice
and Charlie Fitka from Marshall—stayed in the mine cabins and
met in the Penzes' home for study and meals.

After a lovely, peaceful white Christmas, Dave and Vera

prepared for their first deputation trip as a couple. They left daughter Dianne and a married couple, Rick and Becky Lucia, to watch over Kako's affairs while they traveled through the Lower 48, raising support and sharing their vision for the retreat center.

They returned to busy days with flights to visit people in nearby villages. As the Penzes listened to the villagers' stories and requests about when they could come to retreats, they saw more strongly than ever the need for a place like Kako Retreat Center. Dave overhauled equipment and worked on plumbing, anticipating the arrival of son Jonathan and other summer help.

Back to the Itinerant Ministry

By mid-October 1989, snow blanketed Kako again, and temperatures fell to the 20s. In their continuing itinerant ministry, Dave and Vera were led to people who most needed their encouragement. In one small village, they talked to a woman who'd recently returned to drinking after being sober for eight years. She hated what she was doing, and as they prayed with her, she asked the Lord's forgiveness and made a new start.

In Grayling, Dave conducted a funeral service for one of two teenagers who had drowned in the Yukon River. His words greatly comforted the Christian parents, and Dave shared the Good News of the gospel at the service.

In the village of Shageluk, they visited a mother who had three small children and was dying of cancer. She told them that she had trusted Christ as her Savior and was ready to go home to heaven. They prayed and sang hymns with her, and shortly after they left, she passed away.

In the larger village of Bethel, the Penzes used a taxi to get from place to place. Dave recognized the young woman driving them as having attended Camp Inowak on the Kuskokwim. She asked them to pray for her marriage and asked, "When can I come for a retreat?"

Dave's Vision for Kako Retreat Center

Dave had a clear vision for completing the retreat center. In his imagination, he pictured it spread in a rectangle over the hill beside the airstrip. Along the creek next to the airstrip and also up the left side of the rectangle, they would build staff houses, adding to the number as needed. One of those houses would be a home for him and Vera that could be wired for electricity. Then their old mining cabin could serve as temporary headquarters for retreats.

On the right side of the rectangle, they'd build tiers of campers' cabins. At the top of the slope, between staff houses and cabins, would sit the washhouse with showers, sinks, and toilets. There would be laundry facilities on the lower floor. And someday, a big lodge would rise next to the washhouse, with an office, meeting space, and bookstore on the second floor and a commercial kitchen and dining room to seat 50 people on the first floor. There would also be a building to use as a gold lab, and a hangar would be built for the airplane. The hangar would include a heated shop so projects could continue throughout the cold months.

Dianne drew a charming pen-and-ink sketch of her father's vision. Over the years, as the retreat center was developed, it ended up looking remarkably like that first sketch, and the Penzes constantly acknowledged it was the prayers and support of God's people around the country that made it all possible.

Dave and Vera in 1988 in front of their first home at Kako
Credit: Vera Penz

Vera Penz and Debbie Holland in their kuspuks,
summer parkas made by the Eskimo women
Credit: Joan Husby

Kako Retreat Center from the air. Lodge and washhouse are lower right, two rows of campers' cabins at left and staff houses, far right and along runway. Shops, hangar and other buildings along top of photo. Canoe pond and garden spot center.
Credit: Cody Ramirez

Dinnertime at the 2013 Ladies' Berry Picking Retreat, dining room in Hooley Lodge
Credit: Joan Husby

Jeanne Rodkey speaking to a group of campers in Hooley Lodge
Credit: Joan Husby

Teen Campers on Kako's climbing wall and rappeling tower built by John Erickson
Credit: John Erickson

Gordon Bakke with a plane-load of
supplies for Kako
       Credit: Gordon Bakke

Pastor George Landlord cleaning salmon
       Credit: Gordon Bakke

Dave Penz and friend panning Kako gold
       Credit: Gordon Bakke

CHAPTER 17
Building through Prayer

Keeping the Main Thing the Main Thing

Vera always began their prayer letters with praise to God for blessings. In letters over succeeding years, she highlighted events through which their partners could see the development of Kako Retreat Center in answer to prayer. She included the hard work, the adventure, the joys and sorrows that were part of daily life at Kako, and also chronicled the hearts that were changed by Christ's love.

Through it all, they endeavored to live out the motto they'd appropriated from a bumper sticker: "Keep the main thing the main thing." To them, the main thing always meant reaching Alaska's Native peoples with the Good News about Jesus. To that end, prayer requests in 1990 included safe air travel and wisdom in decision making during "iffy" weather. A weekend retreat planned for two schoolteacher families from Akiak had to be rescheduled due to snow and poor visibility. Such rescheduling often happened during the winter months.

But sometimes the weather allowed a window for a trip they feared might be canceled, as when Dave and Vera flew to Anchorage for a board meeting late in January. Fog the previous day had grounded all small planes. But the day of the meeting dawned clear and cold, allowing them to get to Anchorage. The following day, fog prevented their return home. That was fine with Vera.

She'd not been in town for nearly three months and reveled in the extra opportunity for shopping and Christian fellowship.

Identifying Needs

In February 1990, three missionaries from SEND North spent a few days with the Penzes while carrying out a demographic study of villages in Western Alaska. They found Kako's surroundings to be the most spiritually needy area in the entire state.

Not only was there a lack of Christ-centered churches—or even a Christian witness in many of the villages—but drugs and alcohol also tore homes apart and caused much suffering. These findings only increased Dave and Vera's urgency to share the gospel in the Yukon-Kuskokwim Delta. They continually requested prayer for open doors in the surrounding villages and that they might be able to connect with and encourage key families. Villagers always found a warm welcome when they visited Kako, and the friendships formed led to more opportunities for evangelism.

In her letters to supporters, Vera requested prayer that God would call couples to come alongside as staff. But she knew that answering such a call entailed much sacrifice. Not only did staff members have to raise all their own support, but they would also live an isolated, rural lifestyle. Their children would have to be homeschooled, an educational solution for which not every parent was equipped.

Most men found life at Kako exciting and satisfactory because they were busy outside, enjoyed the hunting, and had the fellowship of coworkers. It was harder for their wives. Some women enjoyed the challenge of Kako, but others felt intensely lonely and isolated. This greatly shortened the tenure of some staff families. Other couples were motivated by the vision of taking the gospel to Western Alaska's Native peoples, no matter the hardships. Those staff members adapted well, especially if they were already accustomed to a rural lifestyle, and some moved into the villages to live among and serve the Natives there.

Construction Begins

In 1990, construction began on the hill above the old mine buildings. In only two weeks, a six-person work team from Little Genesee, New York, raised the walls, trusses, and roof of the first staff house and completed the basement and floor of the second. They put room partitions inside the first house and installed wiring. In September, a team that included Dave's daughter Valerie, installed insulation and drywall in the first home and raised the walls, trusses, and roof for the second.

Volunteers Tom and Mae Minter joined the team, with Mae helping Vera. The two women figured that in September they had fed up to 11 people a total of 587 meals. Tom Minter helped with construction and then ran electric power to the new buildings. Dave and Vera were thrilled to look up the hill to their future home and see electric lights.

Meanwhile, when Dave and Jonathan weren't helping with construction, they worked at the mining site. Although they had to spend much of their time on equipment repairs, they did find some gold. And because the first two weeks of October were unusually warm, the men were able to continue mining a bit longer than usual, enabling them meet part of Kako's financial needs.

Dave hoped to continue supporting the retreat center through his gold-mining endeavors, but by 1990, he and Vera were beginning to realize that the Lord was sending sufficient finances through his people across the country. The gifts were enough to cover expenses for retreats and travel to the villages, as well as to purchase building supplies for various construction projects.

Helpers at Home

These supporters were truly partners in the work at Kako—financially, and just as important, by praying. Vera wrote, "My! How we realize the importance of prayer." She quoted James O. Fraser, a missionary to China, who said, "Solid, lasting missionary work is done on our knees." He wasn't referring to just the knees of the missionary but of those in the homeland as well. Fraser continued, "I am feeling more and more that it is, after all, the prayers of God's people that call down blessing upon the work, whether they are directly engaged in it or not... If this is so, then Christians at home can do as much for foreign missions as those actually on the field."[12]

The Yukon-Kuskokwim Delta of Western Alaska is so remote, it might well seem like a foreign country to most Americans. But the Penzes knew that neither distance nor obstacles can limit the power of prayer.

Kako Retreat Center Takes Shape

That winter, work on the staff houses progressed, with insulation, drywall installation and taping, painting, plumbing, and cabinets.

In the spring of 1991, Dave and Vera moved into the partially finished staff house number one. Partitions were removed in the old mining cabin they'd been living in to create one large lounge and dining area, and the former bedroom was turned into a kitchen in what was now KRC's multipurpose building.

With the help of volunteers, the two staff houses were painted, and work began on the first three camper cabins. Volunteers also cut and stockpiled logs, landscaped the grounds, planted grass, weeded the garden, and helped in the kitchen. That summer a radio-phone was installed, making it possible at last for Kako to communicate directly with the outside world. Dave and Vera were encouraged, not only by the work the volunteers accomplished, but also that many of them pledged to pray for them and Kako's ministry.

Peter Egelak, a young man who often stayed at Kako, became a dependable helper. His parents had been alcoholics. One time, when Peter and his three siblings were young, they saw his father

12 Geraldine Taylor, *Behind the Ranges: The Life-Changing Story of J. O. Fraser* (OMF Books, 1998).

beat his mother for five hours. No one came to help her, and she died. The father was imprisoned, but after his release, he shot another man in anger and then turned the gun on himself.

His children had to live with those memories, and not surprisingly, they tried to hide the pain by drinking. The Penzes worked with all four siblings, but Peter stayed at Kako the most. He was able to stop drinking, and in later years he carried on a ministry of his own, counseling and helping alcoholics in the villages.

After 1991's busy June and July, Dave and Jonathan, along with Peter Egelak and Wilbert Nicholas, concentrated on the mining work.

That winter, families from the surrounding villages of Marshall, Russian Mission, Akiak, Bethel, Grayling, and Holy Cross came to enjoy weekend retreats. They stayed in the 55-year-old mining cabins and met together in the renovated multipurpose building for meals and classes.

CHAPTER 18
More Warfare, More Victories

God's Protecting Hand

In early 1992, Dave and Vera left on a trip of over 14,000 miles by plane, automobile, and Amtrak train to visit family, friends and supporters in the Lower 48. While driving a rental car on the busy beltway surrounding Chicago, their lives and ministry nearly came to a premature end on the afternoon of February 27.

The driver of a large semi-truck didn't see them and swung into their lane. His front bumper hooked their left rear fender, flinging them in front of the truck. Their vehicle went airborne across three lanes of traffic. As they flew over the truck, Dave caught a glimpse of its radiator cap. They plunged head-on toward the cement divider, but inexplicably turned 90 degrees in midair, almost parallel with the barrier. Instead of crossing over the divider into oncoming 70-mile-per-hour traffic, a front wheel hit the wall. The car slid down and along the wall for about 20 feet.

Although their lives were spared, the car was totaled. Vera's chest and back were injured by her seat belt, and Dave, who had braced himself, hit his shoulder and head and broke a chip out of his knee-cap. He hurt from head to toe. Neither had broken bones, but they were sore for weeks.

Despite the accident happening in broad daylight on a busy freeway, no witnesses came forward. The trucker's insurance company denied his involvement in the accident and refused to cover expenses.

Work and Fun

The next month, home again after the accident and recovering from their injuries, the Penzes hosted Native couples who came from several villages for a weekend with an InterAct missionary. Some were the only believers in their communities, so the teaching and fellowship greatly encouraged them.

The last week in May brought one problem after another. The power generator quit, there were problems with the airplane and the water line, Dave came down with bronchial pneumonia, and Vera's oven quit working. "We are in spiritual warfare," Vera wrote to their supporters. "But in all of these circumstances, we realize God is in control. Join us in prayer and then rejoice as God gives victory."

They worked through the problems, with much expense and prayer. Most of the summer was sunny and dry, perfect for construction projects and mining. Volunteers painted the three cabins and readied them for floor coverings. They framed in a new washhouse and put on the roof.

In July 1992, Jeanne's family, plus the rest of the Penz children—Valerie, Dianne, and Jonathan—joined the Penzes at the center. For the first time in four years, all were together in a happy reunion. While there, John Rodkey and their friend Anne set up Kako's first computer and programmed it to meet the ministry's needs.

Births, weddings, and funerals in the surrounding villages continued to give them opportunities to be involved in the lives of the people they cared about. They looked ahead to winter conferences, especially an October workshop for men on the topic of being good fathers.

Due to a critical need for more help in the work they were trying to do, Dave and Vera were excited to tell supporters of a new family applying to serve as associates at Kako. Grant and Lenna Funk, both Bible college graduates, along with their five children, hoped to join them as full-time staff. Grant, a registered emergency medical technician and Lenna, a registered nurse, had lived in Northern Canada, as well as in the village of Anaktuvuk Pass in Northern Alaska, so they were used to the bush. They also homeschooled their children. The family bought an older model travel trailer to live and travel in while they raised the funds needed to support themselves at Kako.

At Christmastime, Dave and Vera were alone at the retreat center. Since Jonathan was working at Bethel, Dave had made several attempts to fly to there to bring him and two friends back for the holidays. Each time he tried, snow, fog, and ice forced him to turn back.

At 6:00 on Christmas morning, before Dave had started the generator, the lights came on! What had happened? Then they heard a snow machine pull up to the front door. To the Penzes' delight, there stood Jonathan and his friends! They had driven all night—about 100 miles—to arrive in time for the holiday.

Later in the day a Native couple from Russian Mission, Martha and Moses Gabrieloff, also arrived by snow machine. They were among several families from that village who often borrowed Christian videos to watch. This time they came to help celebrate Christmas.

In February 1993, Vera and Martha made a trip to Anchorage to attend the Native Musicale. Vera enjoyed seeing old friends from across the state. She also had dental work done and did some necessary shopping. While she was gone, Dave cleared four feet of packed snow off the runway.

Materials for kitchen and bathroom cabinets for both staff houses awaited assembly. Dave Peterson, a cabinetmaker with MARC (Missionary Aviation Repair Center), came to do that job in time for the arrival of the Funk family.

Narrow Escape and God's Provision

Women from distant villages, as well as from closer communities, were hoping to come to a ladies retreat scheduled for March 26–28. Dave and Vera flew to Russian Mission on March 6 to distribute retreat flyers, then returned to Kako. As they taxied through some packed snow to park the plane, metal fatigue caused a landing gear leg, which connected a wheel to the plane, to break off next to the fuselage. If their speed had been any greater, the plane would have crashed. The Penzes weren't hurt, but the plane's propeller and a wing received substantial damage.

Two pilot friends happened to be at the center. They helped the Penzes climb out of the plane and assisted in other ways. But the Penzes' main means of transportation was out of commission. They carried insurance only on passengers. All of their finances had gone into building KRC and the ministry, so they had no money to cover the estimated $9,000 to $10,000 it would cost to repair the 40-year-old plane. Was this the time for the newer, larger plane they needed? Vera sent out a prayer SOS.

Normally an entire month would be needed to make the repairs, and already retreats at Kako had been planned for March and April. The Penzes asked for prayer for God's direction and wisdom, for finances, and for another airplane to fill in while they waited for theirs to be repaired.

Those prayers were answered as people sent financial gifts and letters of encouragement. Spencer and Carolyn Lyman, friends at Snow Gulch, allowed them to use Carolyn's Cessna 172 while the Penzes' plane was being repaired. Women left the ladies' retreat refreshed and encouraged, and on the next day, March 29, the seven-member Funk family flew into Russian Mission, then drove the rest of the way by snow machine. The oldest child, Christy, was a teenager, with the rest of the children stair-stepping down in age to the youngest, a toddler.

"God's timing is perfect," Vera exulted. The Funks arrived just in time to help with the next retreats. On March 31 and again on April 6, Kako hosted students from Russian Mission and Marshall, 45 teenagers in all. They came for school-sponsored seminars on drug and alcohol abuse. Kako provided the facilities, meals, and some activities. The Easter weekend retreat for teachers followed.

On May 26, Dave and a friend flew to Port Alsworth to pick up their repaired Cessna 180. They still owed $4,000, but they had their wings back.

Summer 1993 flew by in a whirl of activities, entertaining weekend guests, visiting in the villages, and attending meetings in Anchorage. The Funk family prepared a lovely, candlelight dinner for two for Dave and Vera's fifth wedding anniversary. A few days later, Christy Funk accompanied Vera to Bethel where Vera spoke at a mother-daughter luncheon. Over 100 attended. Dave flew on to Sleetmute and Stony River, where he spoke at Stony River's high school graduation ceremony and visited with old friends.

Sharing in the Dream

In the three campers' cabins, beds were built and linoleum and carpet tiles laid. Work was finished just in time for the arrival of a team of 16 retired people from Pennsylvania who worked on the washhouse and an intercom system, plus sawing lumber, painting, cooking, and whatever else needed to be done. Other helpers remodeled a bunkhouse and reroofed one of the mining cabins, and Peter Egelak returned to help with the mining.

Early in August, Deb and her family arrived for two weeks. One Sunday, while KRC was buzzing with guests and volunteer helpers, three young men wearing backpacks approached on the runway. The strangers were from Switzerland and Germany. They were headed for the Bering Sea and had already kayaked and canoed 1,800 miles on the Yukon River from Whitehorse, Yukon Territory.

Their map showed Kako as an abandoned mine, so they were astonished to see all the people, plus a working mine. They gladly joined the group for dinner and their Sunday service, at which Grant Funk gave the clear plan of salvation. After staying overnight, they hiked back to the Yukon River and their canoes.

Later in August, the Penzes rejoiced that not only had finances come in to cover repairs on their Cessna 180, but that the Funks now owned a Cessna 172 to use in the ministry. Grant had returned to Minnesota to take flying lessons. He bought the plane and flew it to Kako with an instructor, accumulating the flying hours he needed for his private pilot's license.

At the end of 1993, Kako's prayer letter was filled with thanks to God: praise for Dave's spiritual refreshment at a missions conference in Canada, for the many coming to Kako for fellowship and spiritual help, and for the extra assistance in completing many projects, including several people who worked through the winter months.

On April 14, 1994, Dave flew to Anchorage for surgery on the shoulder that had been injured in the traffic accident while they were on deputation in 1992. Two weeks after that, he and Vera had to be at a location in Indiana, near Chicago, to give a deposition.

The following year, nearly four years after the accident, Dave was summoned to Indiana again to meet with their lawyer and then to attend a mediation at Christmastime. He and Vera agreed to settle out of court for $15,000, which covered only about half of their expenses. Though the settlement was far less than they'd hoped for, they were thankful to see the ordeal end.

CHAPTER 19
Growth in the Century's Final Decade

Staff Members

Over the years, many people, both single and married, applied to serve on staff. Some served for several years until the Lord led them elsewhere. Others realized that they were not well-fitted for the primitive, isolated conditions and didn't stay long.

When the Funk family came on board in 1992, it was a blessing in many ways. With so many people coming and going, having a second pilot and plane at camp helped greatly. That winter, along with Dave and Vera, the Funk family, and additional helpers, the number of full-time residents at Kako swelled to 15.

The Funk family added much to the life of the center. Grant's airplane ministry to the villages kept him busy. When the Penzes made their annual winter trip to visit supporting churches and friends in the Lower 48, the Funks kept the home fires burning and carried on the ministry.

Time for the Lodge

In 1995, work finally began on the long-anticipated Ed Hooley Lodge. After a second successful youth rally that summer with 26 teenagers from several villages in attendance, the staff all agreed that they needed more room.

By October, the process was underway, due to the Lord's unexpected provision of funds. Ella Mae Hooley, Ed Hooley's sister, had been saving money to come to Kako. When she passed into heaven, her family bequeathed her entire bank account of over $17,000 to the retreat center. The Penzes, overwhelmed, agreed the funds would provide a good start on the lodge.

Dave ordered materials. They were barged up the Yukon, and when the trail to the river froze, they were hauled by truck to Kako and stored until construction could start in the spring.

In 1996, the Penzes received 100 copies of the *Jesus* film. Excited about this new method of evangelism, they began distributing the film to key homes in the villages.

In May they held their first Leadership Training School, followed by a second session in the fall. These were established to train Christians for leadership positions in their local churches and/or villages. Ten men from five villages attended the first school, a life-changing time for them. One man said, "We came here weak and we went away strong." Some followed up by enrolling in Bible correspondence courses.

Back-to-back work teams were lined up from late May through August to help build the lodge and two cabins. Sixty-one people from six different states—Wisconsin, Colorado, Minnesota, Pennsylvania, California, and Alaska—came to help

The Funk family, who'd just moved into the newly finished, more spacious third staff house, spent much of March and April in Palmer awaiting the arrival of baby number six. On March 28, Lenna gave birth to 10-pound Lydia Olivia, who delighted everybody at the center.

Within days of receiving a prayer letter telling of the need for help in bringing in saw logs for summer projects, Mark Sorenson, a logger from Ketchikan, and Verlin Hoffman, also from Alaska, both arrived in early March. Mark, Verlin, and Dave, along with Bill Wilson, a pilot and mechanic who'd just arrived with his wife and two small children for a four-month stay, became a great team, cutting and bringing in over 300 saw logs by snow machine and loader. Now they could begin making the lumber for two more cabins, the lodge, and a woodworking shop.

LIVING GOLD

That summer of 1996, using lumber cut from the winter's harvest of logs, teams completed the shells of two additional camper cabins, plus the woodworking shop. They also raised the 28-x-48-foot, two-story Ed Hooley Lodge. The Penzes looked to the Lord and their supporters to provide another $20,000 to enclose the lodge for winter. Their goal was to complete the building in time for a dedication the following spring.

For a second year, weather and equipment breakdowns made it impossible to mine, but the Lord made up for the lost income in other ways. Kako fed and housed a team of geologists for two weeks in 1996, which helped pay the bills. Supporters gave sacrificially and the work continued.

Although the years following 1996 had their share of challenges, Kako also experienced times of harvest after years of seed sowing. Teen camps were filled to overflowing, with excellent counselors including some Native people. A good number of young people made decisions to follow Christ and many other youth received encouragement and instruction. As the camps increased in attendance and popularity, the Penzes were thrilled to see many teens and younger kids take a stand for Christ.

In late May 1997, Pennsylvania volunteers came to work on the lodge, as well as help in hosting a three-week training course in Home Care for women from villages. The Pennsylvanian team's home church had asked for a wish-list of items needed for the lodge and new cabins. The congregation sent a treasure trove of dishes, glassware, baking pans, towels, linens, blankets, pillows, and bedspreads.

Camp buzzed with activity while everyone prepared for an open house and lodge dedication planned for July 5 and 6. The Funk family returned after almost six months of traveling in a Greyhound bus that had been converted to a motor home, as they shared about Kako and raised support. In mid-June, nine pilots and mechanics from the Cornerstone Aviation Program came to Kako to work on the planes. Pilot Bill Wilson accompanied the group and stayed through the dedication. A team of California volunteers worked up until the night before, getting the lodge ready.

Fifty-nine friends and family members—including Dave's elderly mother and father, as well as three of Dave's four children— came from near and far to be part of the celebration. They rejoiced together as they sang, "To God be the glory, great things he hath done!"

Dave recounted Ed Hooley's vision of a retreat center to serve the people of the Y-K Delta. He told how the dream had seemed to perish with Ed and Joyce in that 1977 airplane crash and how God used other people and circumstances to bring the vision to pass. Gale Van Diest of InterAct Ministries spoke of his own excitement and zeal for the ministry, encouraging all.

One family came by boat and camped in a tent. Relatives of both Ed and Joyce Hooley were deeply touched to see their loved ones' dream now a reality.

The new lodge was put to use within a few weeks during a teen retreat for 26 young people from surrounding villages. The beautiful weather allowed the kids to swim in the canoe pond. They ate and held meetings in the lodge and marveled at the new space. Grant Funk headed up the retreat, the theme of which was "Make up your mind! Take a stand!"

"Be consistent!" Grant told the kids. "Your one life could influence 10,000 people." Six boys accepted Christ during the retreat, and others signed up for correspondence Bible studies.

Ministering to Young People

On Eagles Wings, a ministry made up of Ron Hutchcraft and 18 Native Americans trained to minister to other Native teens, spent a week at the August 1998 teen camp at Kako. They also traveled to a number of villages: Mountain Village, St. Mary's, Hooper Bay, Marshall, and Holy Cross, as well as the larger towns of Bethel and Kodiak.

First, they held a leadership training session. Three of Kako's Native people attended and became part of the team. In each village, On Eagles Wings held meetings in the school gym, with basketball, skits, music, and pizza. The evenings ended with team members telling how Christ had changed their lives. Then they witnessed to the young people one on one. Hundreds of those young people signed cards indicating their desire to follow Christ. Immediately, Kako people got involved in follow-up and discipleship. The follow-up program continued in the villages the next year as well. During the summer months the group flew to other states with their outreach.

Ongoing Obstacles, Ongoing Ministry

In December 1997, Bill and Wanda Wilson came on staff, and Bill used their own plane in their ministry.

In January 1998, a gathering of Native Men for Christ, scheduled to be held in Mountain Village, was almost thwarted by snow so heavy that small plane flights were canceled. The speakers and singers flew by commercial plane to nearby St. Mary's, then snow-machined through a blizzard to Mountain Village. Visitors from the surrounding area also came by snow machine. One family spent seven hours on the trail to reach the gathering.

In February and March, two men's workshops were held. One man who had attended Kako's very first retreat nine years earlier had accepted the Lord and now shared his faith with others. Sandwiched between the men's workshops was a retreat for women. Then the day before the Easter Teacher's Retreat, Kako staffers woke up to a blizzard. The pilots couldn't fly to pick up the 48 teachers and their families, so Dave radio-phoned to postpone the retreat until the following weekend. A smaller group of people came than was originally planned. Still it was a time of blessing, marked by the testimonies of a recently converted couple.

Next, pilots brought in 43 people from surrounding villages to attend a Grieving Native Seminar with Art and Elizabeth Holmes.

Many were teenagers from communities that had experienced recent suicides. The Penzes were overwhelmed at the response. It made them aware of the great need for such seminars. Art Holmes, the author of the book *The Grieving Indian*, was invited, along with his wife, to hold more seminars in six villages.

Dave had long dreamed of holding gold-prospecting workshops for the surrounding villagers. In mid-May, a geologist from Calista Corporation, one of 13 Alaska Native Regional Corporations created under the Alaska Native Claims Settlement Act of 1971, came to Kako and held classes each morning. Dave provided hands-on experience as attendees enthusiastically hiked to the creeks to practice what they'd learned. His hope was that prospecting could provide another way for Native people to support themselves. The Natives' enthusiasm opened doors for further contact, and some of the men brought their families back for the 1998 Memorial Day Family Retreat.

In June, strong, gusting tailwinds blew Dave off the runway, and the crash totaled his plane. He wasn't hurt, and he did carry insurance on the plane, but being without a plane that summer limited his ministry.

Rain, fog, and high winds canceled that year's August Berry Picking Retreat. In mid-September, the women were finally able to attend a ladies' retreat, and they experienced a joyful time of fellowship, culminating with the salvation of a close friend for whom the Penzes had been praying. The fall teacher's retreat was well attended, and a schoolteacher put her trust in the Lord.

But then, Dave took off in the plane belonging to Grant Funk to take three teachers home. The plane hit a microburst downdraft and crashed into evergreens, just 300 feet beyond the Penzes' home. A tree sheared off a wing and the tail. The plane slid down another tree, landing on all three wheels. The occupants walked away with no serious injuries, but now two planes were out of commission.[13]

13 A microburst is a small intense downdraft, descending at speeds of up to 6000 feet per minute. On nearing the surface, winds spread outward

Weather conditions are frequently a hindrance to Kako's ministry. Satan fights constantly to hold back God's work in the Far North, but the prayers of God's people advance it.

---

in all directions from the downdraft center, causing both vertical and horizontal wind shears that can be extremely hazardous to all types of aircraft, especially at low altitudes. Due to their small size, short life span, and the fact that they can occur even when rain is not reaching the ground, microbursts are not easily detectable using conventional weather radar or wind shear alert systems.

CHAPTER 20
God at Work through Challenges

Growth and Change

While Kako's staff changed over the years, camps and retreats also expanded in attendance. That meant more people to transport, feed, and house. Maintenance of grounds, buildings, airplanes, and equipment had to be carried on. Something was usually under construction.

One such project began in the summer of 1999, when Dave and his helpers excavated for and installed the gravel pad on which the much-needed airplane hangar would be erected. They planned to raise the building after the ground froze. Pilots and mechanics alike looked forward to warm storage for the airplanes, as well as a place to work on them.

Much other work also had to be completed before winter set in. The men were busy digging a water line to the newest staff house, 12 feet deep to protect the pipes from freezing. The Penzes' unfinished basement still needed a wooden floor and proper drainage. The center's supply of firewood needed to be brought in and cut. All those jobs depended on volunteers.

Also in 1999, a work team from North Carolina brought their chainsaws and cleared trees and brush to extend the airstrip's length to 2600 feet. The strip has a seven-degree slope with a curve at the 2000-foot mark, so take-offs and landings must be done with special care.

Training Leaders

The start of the new millennium brought successful and well-attended retreats, workshops, and camps for young people. For a video series called *Born to Fly*, 27 men came from surrounding villages. One man testified that earlier in the week, he'd had a rifle in his mouth, ready to pull the trigger. At that moment, his telephone rang. Grant Funk was calling to invite him to the men's workshop. He put away his rifle, attended the workshop, and went home a changed man.

The Leadership Training Institute began in the year 2000. The first course, entitled "Introduction to the Unity of the Bible," attracted seven enthusiastic students, mostly men. Six more classes were scheduled for the winter and spring. Dave hoped these classes would eventually be expanded into a Bible school adapted to the cultural factors unique to life on the Yukon-Kuskokwim Delta.

One of these unique factors is that life in roadless areas is very different than life where automobiles are a necessity. Most younger adults have responsibilities for older family members that make it hard to be away from the village for more than two or three days at a time. Younger people check the fishnets for Grandma and Grandpa every few days, watch after them, and make sure they have firewood beside their door. So pilots from Kako picked students up around 4:00 p.m. on Friday, when those who have jobs are usually finished. They'd have classes for a couple of hours on Friday, 10 hours on Saturday, and on Sunday for four or five hours, then go home.

Ups, Downs, and Challenges

More than 100 volunteer workers came to Kako during the summer of 2001. They helped with youth camps, built another cabin and staff house number six—which could also serve as a dormitory for the Leadership Training Institute—painted many of the buildings, and did outside electrical work. They started a second hangar and completed the attached shop building. The new Wood-Mizer portable sawmill made cutting lumber easier and faster.

The second attempt at building an airplane hangar could not be finished before winter set in. Heavy wet snow again collapsed the arches. This time, fortunately, no plane was underneath. The men repurposed the salvaged corrugated metal to build storage sheds needed around camp, and drew up plans to try again. The hangar was over 100 feet long, with a tin roof at a nine-to-12 pitch to shed snow. One side was used to work on the planes, and the other side was used for storage.

In 2002, Vera's daughter Debbie Holland and her family came for the Christmas holiday to enjoy a working vacation, with plenty of play in the snow. On December 22, someone looked out a window and noticed black smoke pouring from the generator shed. Then the building burst into flames. As people came running, the flames spread to the wood shop next door. Working together, the group was able to save most of the shop's equipment, although airplane parts, tools, and lumber stored in the loft went up in flames.

They lost both generators and had no electricity for five days, but they dug out kerosene lanterns and candles and enjoyed meals by candlelight until Dave and one of the men hooked up another generator to provide partial power. They heard about someone in Minnesota who wanted to sell a Cummins 40 KW generator. It was delivered, freight free, to Russian Mission, where Dave and helpers loaded it onto a sled. They pulled the heavy generator with two snow machines to Kako Landing. From there they used their Caterpillar to pull it the last six miles to Kako. They housed the generator in a van, and soon Kako had power again.

It turned out that the oil lines vibrate when the generator is operating. If a line develops a crack or hole, the fuel oil can vaporize and fill the building with fumes. If the fumes hit something hot, they explode. That is what happened to cause the fire.

Because fire safety is always a big concern in a place like Kako, automatic sprinkler systems have been installed near the furnaces to decrease risk in the staff houses. The homes were built 28 feet apart to prevent the spread of flames from one house to the next should one of them burn.

The 2003 retreats, camps, and workshops were well attended. Many lives changed as a result of the Good News being proclaimed. Eight young first-timers at Kako came from the town of Pilot Station to attend snow camp. During summer camps, over 40 young people prayed to receive Christ, and 10 women received Christ at the Ladies' Berry Picking Retreat. Afterward, Bible correspondence courses helped them to grow in their faith at home.

Also that year, three women from Kako flew to Akiak to organize a kids' club. Fifty children attended, and several received Christ. Then in October, Kako hosted a Moravian Pastors' and Elders' Conference for over 40 pastors and elders from 21 surrounding villages. They sang, prayed, and testified in their Yupik dialect and were challenged to more effective ministries, especially for reaching young people in their communities.

The next summer's camping program added more sessions for a total of six weeks, attracting 160 young people from 19 villages. Fifty-three of them made decisions for Christ.

Peter Egelek, a longtime helper at Kako, spent 10 months in Florida taking a training course dealing with drug and alcohol abuse. He then stayed another 10 months training as a teacher and learned how to utilize the materials as part of Kako's ministry. Upon his return, he set up a program for those recovering from addictions. He frequently traveled to the villages to share his own experiences. Eventually, he married Lucy Green from Hooper Bay and brought her to Kako, along with two of her daughters. Later, the family moved to Hooper Bay where he carried on his ministry.

Victor Ladeira, who had flown part-time at Kako for a number of years, came on staff full time to take charge of airplane maintenance, ATVs, radios, and computers. One of his projects was to overhaul the engine and perform the annual inspection on the Cessna 206. He was done in time for the busy summer camping season. The Penzes especially appreciated Victor's help when in November 2004, Dave had a TIA (transient ischemic attack, or ministroke). Fortunately the stroke did not prove to have lasting consequences, but Federal Aviation Administration regulations prevented him from flying until FAA doctors gave their approval.

In 2005, Jerry and Delores Gardner, after seven years of faithful service on the staff, retired to their home in Michigan. Gary and Margo Posenjak, who had helped in the camping program for three summers, became a permanent part of the staff in 2006. Gary became Director of Camping Ministries and pastor for Kako.

In 2006, Dave finally received approval from the FAA to fly again. The Penzes once more pointed out in their letter to supporters the power of prayer in protecting pilots and passengers through the many hours of flying.

In November, Dave had been aloft near Bethel when, just three miles from town, his plane's carburetor iced up. The engine quit, but because of a strong headwind, he was able to set the plane down on the tundra as if landing a helicopter, with no damage to the plane or himself. He'd been talking to the tower in Bethel during the emergency. They sent a snow machine to pick him up. Dave hired a helicopter to ferry the plane to Bethel. He warmed it up in the hangar where he checked it over, then flew it safely home to Kako after determining there was no damage.

In 2006, Sheldon and Cyndy Sharp and their little ones became temporary missionaries on loan to Kako. The board approved the missionary appointment of pilot Mike Boettcher and his wife Cayla, a nurse. Many individuals and teams came to work on summer projects, including a team from New Hyde Park Baptist in New York, a church that had faithfully supported Vera and then Kako for 52 years.

George and Eunice Landlord left Kako to minister in Marshall, where they'd worked previously. After they started a Bible study, villagers packed their house, and a number of people put their trust in the Lord. Eventually, the Samaritan's Purse organization helped to build a church in Marshall, and the Landlords became the first pastors.

Also in 2006, Dave was diagnosed with low-grade chronic lymphocytic leukemia. Doctors began blood monitoring every three months to determine if and when treatment would be needed.

Financial Challenges

Financial challenges have always been a part of the ministry at Kako and require a careful balancing of expenditures and contributions. When energy prices soared from about 2003 through 2008, the spike resulted in increased expenses for aviation gas and diesel fuel. At the same time, Kako's ministry outreach also increased. Higher fuel costs were met by carefully planning all flying to minimize aircraft expenses. Also, Kako put on hold the work on some much needed facilities, such as the airplane hangar and the Leadership Training Institute facility. They put off repaying the large interest-free loan the Penzes had earlier made to the center from their retirement funds. The loan was an emergency measure taken when the barge company refused to offload the winter's aviation gas and diesel fuel unless the cost was prepaid.

Small amounts were later repaid on the loan, but other pressing obligations shoved complete repayment to the bottom of the list. However, the Lord sent needed funds through supporters. After a lifetime of trusting the Lord to provide and finding him faithful, Dave and Vera, as always, left their future in God's hands.

CHAPTER 21
The Camping Program

God continued to bless the ongoing ministries of Kako through the new millennium's first decade and into the second. Youth camps were well attended, as was the family camp held each Memorial Day weekend. The usual retreats and workshops touched many lives.

At first, Dave did not immediately foresee how God would work through the summer camps to change lives among Native young people. He felt that working with the adults was more important. He believed that once they had experienced salvation for themselves and had grown in their Christian walk, they would be able to reach and teach their children at home.

Soon, however, parents begged for camps for their children. The summer camps are primitive compared to camping programs in more affluent areas of the country, but part of Dave's genius lay in adapting activities to suit conditions in Alaska and also in enlisting the aid of gifted, enthusiastic, energetic directors and counselors.

Reaching Alaska's Native Kids Through Camping

John Erickson has spent a number of summers as Kako's summer camp activities director, as well as filling in wherever work needs doing.

Like at any Christian camp, kids are offered stories, music, crafts, and times to learn about God. Directors and cabin leaders also keep kids busy with such new and exciting activities as a pool, archery, paintball, canoeing, and an obstacle course. There's also a shooting range to learn marksmanship and gun safety. Every summer John tried to add something different for the kids. In 2009, he designed a temporary rappelling wall on a gravel bluff. The following year he built a sturdy, more complex climbing and rappelling tower. It takes a lot of faith to lean back into space with only a rope to keep one from falling. Young people must learn to depend upon the helpers and to trust the rope. Once past that frightening, initial letting go, the campers love the activity. John would tell them that trusting the rope is like trusting Jesus. It may seem really hard, but the result is worth it.

Another example of a trust-building activity is an "Alaskan obstacle course," built outdoors from whatever resources are handy. Kids might help build a low bridge with loose sticks laid along the top. They must wriggle underneath without knocking any off. They next race through a double row of old tires laid on the ground, stepping in each without tripping. They help each other walk a "tightrope" tied 18 inches above the ground, between two trees, or "walk a plank" fashioned from a small log laid atop two stumps.

There's a homemade swing set to play on, and indoor games, relays, and tug-o-wars. Fun is limited only by one's imagination.

Another faithful volunteer, Gordon Bakke, director of the Mission Aviation Training Academy in Arlington, Washington, spent 10 years flying for Kako and interacting with young campers. He remembers one summer when two couples from the Florida Child Evangelism Fellowship held Good News Clubs. During the four weeks of camp, they worked with 160 children, of whom at least 40 gave their hearts to the Lord.

One of those kids was Dalton from Aniak. The village of Aniak had never before sent any of their kids to camp, but Gordon had talked two brothers and their cousin into giving camp a try. Dalton, only 10 but hefty, could not keep up with the others on their exercise run to the cross at the top of the hill. So he walked with a counselor while the other kids ran ahead, and as they walked, Dalton quizzed the counselor about Jesus. Several times on the way, he asked to pray. When they finally reached the top, Dalton knelt at the cross and gave his heart to Jesus. That night he stood in front of the adults and kids and told what had happened. The change in him was apparent to everyone.

Two weeks after he'd gone home, the Kako staff got a call from Dalton's grandmother. "What happened to my boy?" she asked.

The following summer, Aniak sent nine campers. The parents wanted their own kids to experience what Dalton had. Dalton's grandmother happened to work for one of the airlines in Aniak. She persuaded her employer to provide $100 scholarships for the cost of camp. The next year, 30 campers came from that town.

Gordon Bakke concluded that the great need for villagers is the same as for people everywhere—to know the Lord and to have help with their Christian walk.

The Camping Program and Kong Island Camp

More young people kept coming to camp at Kako. As the sessions increased annually in number from four to five to six, and eventually to seven, Dave knew there wasn't enough room at Kako for everyone who wanted to come. He hoped that camps could be set up near other villages.

Among those who shared his vision were three young men, Kyle Stevens, Stephen Weston, and John Erickson. At Kako in 2008, Kyle had led a high school camper from the Kuskokwim River village of Napakiak to the Lord. Eager to share the Good News with his people, the teen asked Kyle to come to Napakiak and help him tell others about Jesus. When Kyle returned to his home, his church prayed with him that the Lord would give him the opportunity to go to the village and encourage his young friend.

During the summer of 2009, a door opened for Kyle Stevens—

now director of the summer camps—and Stephen Weston to go to Napakiak for a week to work with the children. The whole village loved having the young men there, but no one, including Dave, thought a camp for those children was possible that summer.

However, when Kako's camp sessions were over and counselors had mostly returned home, Dave asked Kyle Stevens if he would stay in Alaska and help start a camp on Kong Island, in the Kuskokwim River near Napakiak. Kyle gave an enthusiastic yes. Stephen Weston also agreed to stay longer, and John Erickson returned to help. Camp cook Becky Noll and three other young women, two of them Native, became part of the team. What followed would probably happen only in Alaska, and only with God's help.

By late July, lumber and supplies were ready for the new camp, but weather turned rainy and blustery. No boats were available for transportation to the island. Finally skies cleared, allowing the three men to fly with their tools to Napakiak, 80 miles southwest of Kako. They located a boat to hire. Loading their building supplies aboard, they ferried them across the Kuskokwim River to Kong Island, the site of a fish camp belonging to a village family. The island was close enough to the Bering Sea to be affected by tides, allowing only short periods when boats could get into a slough and land.

The men went to work immediately, clearing away tall grass and fireweed from the space where they wanted to put the camp. The campers could sleep in tents, but they needed a cabin, plus a larger meeting place/kitchen that would be temporarily closed in with plastic. The three worked on building the cabin and the larger building, with John Erickson directing the construction. When they were stranded by weather and tides for a day, they were grateful for the extra time to work.

On the fifth night, someone came to take them to Napakiak. They flew back to Kako to make final preparations and get the rest of the team. They loaded the camp equipment and enough food to feed 25 people for an indefinite period of time. They still didn't know who would come or how long they would stay.

The team arrived back on the island and went right to work. The next day, rain poured down. Wind gusted above 50 miles per hour. Despite the rain—and mosquitoes—they installed a water well and an outhouse, completed construction projects, and set up tents. The children weren't able to come on the day scheduled because of the weather, but next morning someone radioed they were on their way. Everyone rushed around finishing what had to be done and trying to decide what they could get along without.

They heard the kids yelling before they heard the boats—18 excited junior-high-age kids calling the leaders' names as the boats glided in to shore.

The adults greeted the kids, helped them carry their gear to the tents, then fed them lunch. Kyle Stevens said, "It was amazing to see them eating on tables, built that day, in a building built that week."

The campers spent the afternoon rafting in the slough, swimming, painting pictures, playing volleyball and doing other activities. Becky Noll cooked a delicious supper, and then they gathered for a Bible time, with songs, Bible memorization, stories, and a skit.

It rained again on Friday, but even so, the kids had what they called, "an absolute blast." During Bible times, morning and evening, the team shared from Scripture about God's creation, God's power and love, sin and its effects, and God's way of salvation through Jesus Christ.

After the Bible time Friday evening, a 12-year-old boy fell asleep and couldn't completely wake up. He shivered with cold, and his eyes were blank. He appeared to be seeing things that frightened him. The adults realized that Satan was trying to strike fear into the hearts of the young people. They prepared themselves for spiritual warfare. A few staff members stayed behind to pray and sing with the boy, while the rest of the staff took the other kids out to a campfire for a marshmallow roast. One counselor told the 12-year-old about Jesus' love and his power even over demons. The young man gave his life to the Lord that night. When he did, everything he had been seeing fled.

Because of weather and tides, it was necessary for the kids to go home on Saturday morning. Nobody wanted camp to end, but all were excited about coming back and bringing friends from other villages in that area.

Unfortunately, local politics and spiritual powers have so far prevented further efforts at Kong Island, but the need is great, and the story is yet to be finished. Sometimes, as in the case of Kong Camp, it's hard to see what God is doing. Still, it's clear that Kako Retreat Center is being used of God to reach the people of the Yukon-Kuskokwim Delta. Kako is one of his ongoing miracles.

One example of God's blessing is that romance can flourish even in the midst of challenging conditions. That summer of 2009, Becky Noll and John Erickson fell in love and, in 2012, were married. They continue to be an important part of Kako's volunteer staff.

CHAPTER 22
Expanding the Vision

A Call to Harvesters

In 2013, Dave and Vera went to Chicago to attend Founder's Week at Moody Bible Institute. Dave hadn't been back to his old school since 1989. It was there in 1957 that he had begun to think about using his flying skills in missionary work. On this trip he took every opportunity to talk to students about their futures. He told them of the needs in Alaska, hoping that God might use those conversations to call someone to the Northland.

Staffing Needs for the Future

Currently there are eight staff houses for temporary and permanent staff who serve at Kako. Back when Dave first envisioned the buildings the retreat center would need, he realized that as the ministry grew, the need for additional staff would increase. Current needs include:

- A qualified, full-time counselor to deal with depression, abuse, addiction, and other problems in the village, and also to enable Kako to serve as a halfway house for people released from jail.
- At least three couples, based at Kako, who would spend time building relationships with people in the villages. With understanding and a love for Natives as essential qualifications, these couples would stay a night or two with villagers, sleeping on the floor, building friendships

and trust. Under the cover of nighttime, when people are more willing to open up to outsiders about what's on their hearts, missionary couples could then discern where they need help and what they need to know about the message of God's love for them.

- Full-time pilots who could keep two or three airplanes busy all the time. In this roadless area, planes are essential for accessing medical emergencies, grocery and mail runs, and retrieving visitors from Aniak or Bethel, which have larger airfields. They also enable the building of bridges to the far-flung people of the Yukon-Kuskokwim Delta. Sometimes Kako events have to be canceled because no pilot is available to bring people to the retreat center.
- Bible school teachers to train men and women for positions of leadership in the villages. Living quarters will also be needed for these personnel.
- A representative to travel and raise support for Kako.

Volunteers

Kako couldn't run without short-term helpers, such as cooks, pilots, woodcutters, carpenters, housekeepers, clerical help, and directors and counselors for summer camp and winter activities. All of these people serve without pay and must raise money for transportation to Kako.

Cabin leaders are usually young people from Alaskan churches or from the Lower 48. Others, such as teams who come to cut wood or help with construction, donate their vacation time to come and assist. Some, like Jerry and Delores Gardner, are retired. Owners of a maple syrup business in Michigan, the Gardners first came to help for a few weeks in 1995 and ended up spending the winter. They returned every summer for a number of years, going home only in the spring to make maple syrup, some of which they donated to Kako.

In the years since Ed Hooley first dreamed of the retreat center at Kako, hundreds of people have volunteered time and skills. They've given money to support full-time workers or specific projects. Women sewed quilts for the cabins. Others sent books for the library. Airplane repairs were made at discount.

Though relatively few people are privileged to visit Kako, everyone can have a part in the most important support work of all—prayer. People faithfully prayed for those they'd never met and a place they'd never seen.

Some could give only a little, but all was woven together by the mighty power of God to make a place where lives are changed.

The Need for Pilots

Whenever airplanes are down for repairs, friends of Kako often loan a plane and/or offer their flying skills. In the summer of 2013, the Christian Pilots' Association of Alaska loaned one of their planes when Kako's Cessna 182, which is now owned and maintained by Jonathan Penz, went out of service because of a cracked engine casing.

Another group that has provided invaluable help over the years is Mission Aviation Training Academy (MATA), based in Arlington, Washington. This organization trains missionary pilots to serve in fields all over the world. They have often sent planes and pilots to Kako during summer camping season, along with teams of workers who repair Kako's planes and rebuild engines at reasonable prices.

When Jonathan's Cessna 182 needed a complete engine overhaul because of that cracked casing, MATA's maintenance specialist, Dary Finck, took charge of the work. He flew the engine from Kako to Bethel. Lynden Air Transport flew it from Bethel to Anchorage, then trucked it to Fife, Washington. From Fife, Gordon Bakke hauled it to MATA's facility in Arlington.

Many of the needed parts were donated, as was the labor. Donations also paid for most of the freight. Overall, a job like that would ordinarily cost close to $30,000 with the reinstallation. The engine gleamed as if brand new when Lynden Transport returned it to Bethel. From Bethel, Kako's Cessna 206 flew it home. There it was installed in the Cessna 182 by Myron Davis from MATA and volunteers from a local Alaska airline.

MATA's people also help in other essential ways. Executive Director Gordon Bakke and his wife Elaine, a nurse, served as missionaries for 22 years in Zambia, Africa. He joined MATA in 1999, soon after its founding. Gordon got involved with Kako through his friendship with Bob McDowell, who was director of the Free Methodist's Warm Beach Christian Camps and Conference Center, near Arlington. Bob knew the Penzes, and he introduced Dave and Vera to Gordon in 2002 when they came to visit Vera's daughter Debbie, who also lives near Arlington. Dave told Gordon he could use help with flying. Gordon took his first trip to Alaska in the summer of 2002. He fell in love with Kako's ministry and developed a great respect for Dave and Vera.

For seven consecutive summers he flew his Cessna 182 from Arlington to Kako, following the Alaska Highway much of the way. He transported helpers, family camp attendees, and village kids—for four sessions of kids' camp each summer—to and from Kako. He also did the required annual inspections on Kako's aircraft.

Then he sold his Cessna 182 to Mike and Kayla Boettcher, Kako missionaries who now work with MARC (Missionary Aviation Repair Center). The next time Gordon came to Kako, it was as a passenger on a commercial flight. Altogether, he flew at Kako for 10 summers.

All the people at MATA are volunteers. The organization exists on donations. It is not a flight school; rather it is a training program. Each student is on his or her own program, since many also have regular jobs.

For a commercial license, a minimum of 250 flying hours is required. Requirements by mission organizations such as Wycliffe Bible Translators' partner organization JAARS are higher—400 to 500 hours. One way for pilots to earn those hours is to fly for Kako.

Enlarging Hooley Lodge

To handle more people, the Penzes hope to someday add an addition to the front of Hooley Lodge. It will have plenty of indoor plants and large windows to let in sunlight. Upstairs, there will be a nurses' room where kids can lie down if they get sick or hurt. There will be an office room with computers for Bible school students and perhaps a bookstore. The present dining room on the main floor would be extended to seat 100 or more people, eliminating multiple seatings at meals.

Dave's vision included deepening the basement of Hooley Lodge and building a room where kids could learn to make pottery from Kako's pure red clay. A pottery wheel, kiln, and other equipment already reside in a Quonset hut. But without proper heating, it's hard to dry the projects. In the warmth of the proposed pottery room, clay projects would dry evenly and could be fired in time for campers to take their work home. What a way to teach the biblical lesson about clay in the hands of the potter!

A Healthier Way of Life

The healthy subsistence lifestyle in Alaska's bush is fading away. But flown-in groceries are expensive. Fresh fruits and veggies are very limited, although stores do try to offer a variety of frozen goods. Shelves lined with chips, candy, and such snacks tempt old and young alike.

Kako affords opportunities to teach people healthier, better ways of living—physically as well as spiritually. Wild game is used for meals because it's nutritious, available, and much cheaper than beef, pork, or chicken. Vegetables from Kako's garden are served when possible, and some people are now growing gardens in their own villages. Menus at retreats include such Native crowd pleasers as salmon, moose, and even fish-head soup.

Sometimes village women make akutaq (Eskimo ice cream.) They start by squeezing the juice from cooked codfish, then whipping the fish pulp into a bowl of shortening and sugar until fluffy. Then they whip in wild berries for flavor. At almost 500 calories per serving, this is a good energy food for people living in the frigid Far North.

When Jeanne Rodkey, a trained nurse, spoke at 2013's Berry Picking Retreat, she encouraged the women to help their children make good dietary choices. She urged them to keep junk food away from their children as much as possible. "They'll be healthier and do better at school," she said.

A Forward Vision

Looking into the future, one can envision a time when the demons of alcohol, drug addiction and suicide are beaten back by the power of the Holy Spirit. It's a future where villagers are freed to enjoy health, self-respect, and fulfillment in the gifts God gave them. Whether they find that future in the bush or in the city, they will know their value in God's eyes.

CHAPTER 23
A Visionary's Legacy

Seeing the Fruit

Knowing that nothing is lost or wasted in God's economy has helped both of the Penzes to face, with resilience, some of life's most crushing blows. Dave allowed his difficult childhood, his challenging path to education and mission work, and the loss of loved ones—his friends the Hooleys and then of Janet—to become directional signposts on the journey God had for him.

When the leaders at Tatitlek fought hard against the Good News that Al and Vera Kelley tried to bring, when they persecuted new believers, when Vera and her family were shipwrecked in the storm on Prince William Sound, when baby Tommy died in her arms, and when she knew Al had died as well, Vera could have been tempted to believe that they'd misunderstood their calling to the village.

But God had his choice, persevering people. When Tatitlek parents kept young Christians away from the missionaries' influence, some of the youth held on to their faith. The seed that was sown by the Kelleys in the mid-1950s was watered by other missionaries and by Christian schoolteachers. When Vera returned in 1986, 30 years after the shipwreck, she found a Bible chapel established by George Olson and his wife, Leona, who had been two of Vera's Sunday school students before Leona moved with her family to Cordova.

Then, in August 2013, Vera, Debbie, and friend Lynda Jackson enjoyed a trip to the places where Vera had ministered prior to her marriage to Dave: Fairbanks, Glennallen, Copper Center and surrounding communities. Desiring to go to Tatitlek, Vera called the Olsons in Cordova. They told her that the Vlasoffs, who now keep the gospel church in Tatitlek going, were in Valdez. The Vlasoffs took the women in a thirty-foot fishing boat on a three-hour trip across the Sound. When they docked at nearby Ellemar, where the Kelleys had lived, Vera hardly recognized her old community. It now boasts hunting lodges and summer residents. She met two families from Tok whom she had known previously. One family boats over to Tatitlek each week for church.

They attended Sunday morning service, where Vera was presented with the gift of an Alaskan picture, in appreciation for her service there. They also had dinner with the gospel church people. Another visitor to Tatitlek was Virginia, whom Vera had led to the Lord as a child. Still a strong Christian, she was the sister of Jim Paulson, the teenager who was shipwrecked with Vera and Debbie. They also visited Ann Jackson and her husband, the couple who'd been delighted in 1986 to tell Vera about Dave Penz and how Dave had found the Jackson's son Sam wandering aimlessly in Anchorage and introduced him to the Lord. She was thrilled to see God's faithfulness in bringing fruit from the seeds planted during the difficult endeavor at Tatitlek.

Final Flight

During the writing of this book, Dave carefully read each chapter of the draft as it was finished. He offered explanations and additional anecdotes. Thrilled to have the story of God's work at Kako recorded, he looked forward to sharing it with readers. In 2013, when Dave and Vera passed through Washington State on the way to Moody Bible Institute's 60th reunion, the Husbys and the Penzes spent an afternoon together. They visited MATA's headquarters and met with some of the people who'd given such invaluable help to Kako.

Dave continued to think of additions for the book. Although his long-manageable leukemia was getting worse, he was trying a brand-new chemo drug. He said it had helped at least 80 people at Mayo Clinic, and he was feeling better than he had for quite some time. The last time he called, he told a couple of stories and said he had more to share in the next phone call.

A few days later, on April 21, 2014, while Dave was clearing snow from the runway, he became very sick with chills and fever. The next day Vera flew with him to the Veteran's Administration hospital in Anchorage, where he was diagnosed with pneumonia. Dave received oxygen, antibiotics, and two units of blood. Doctors then discovered in his blood the rare and tenacious yeast infection, cryptococcosis. He was given a strong antifungal medication, even though it posed a danger to his kidneys that were functioning at only 40 percent of normal.

On April 27, he was transferred to Alaska Regional Hospital. Doctors told Vera her husband's condition was critical, although they thought it was treatable. Family members gathered. Dave's condition worsened.

The odds in favor of his survival were not good. The family was told that even young people in otherwise good condition are slow to recover from that type of fungal infection. His low immune system almost guaranteed further infections. His diabetes and lifelong lung difficulties added more complications. Doctors predicted that if Dave managed to survive, his recuperation period would last six to 12 months. Even then, he'd have to live in a nursing home and never return to Kako. The only thing keeping him alive was oxygen supplementation. The family debated whether it should be removed. On May 5, Dave's daughter Jeanne e-mailed friends, "It could be today that Jesus will take Dad home."

When several small, encouraging signs gave hope for his temporary improvement, Vera and daughter Debbie returned to Kako to look after critical monthly bills and paperwork, planning to fly back immediately if necessary.

During this time, Native friends and others came to visit Dave. Nurses moved him to a larger room on the hospital's fifth floor. Family and visitors could look out over Merrill field, the site of Dave's innumerable landings and take-offs. At about 10:30 each night, as the family watched the sun's long, slow descent over Mount Susitna, they realized Dave's sun was also setting.

On the morning of May 11, 2014, Vera and Debbie left Kako to return to Dave's side, but 45 minutes before they arrived, his spirit soared out of his suffering body and into the arms of his Savior. Dave's favorite verse, Philippians 1:6, was now fulfilled: "He who began a good work in you will carry it on to completion until the day of Christ Jesus."

Saying Goodbye

Over 150 people attended the funeral service on May 17, 2014, at Anchorage First Baptist Church.

A friend summed up Dave's influence: "Dave had a heart bigger than Alaska." One person after another told about the impact Dave had had on their lives, about his love for God, his faith in difficult circumstances, and his love for Native Alaskans. Later that day, the family held a private ceremony at the cemetery in Palmer and laid Dave's body to rest.

"Dave's work on earth is completed," Vera wrote in her prayer letter the following month, "but the work that he started in the Yukon-Kuskokwim Delta will continue because it is in God's hands, and he is faithful."

Dave's favorite occasion at Kako had always been the family retreat held over Memorial Day weekend. That year, instead of coming to the usual retreat, the family invited people from the villages to a special memorial service for their friend to be held on May 25. Only two of three airplanes were working, so John Rodkey, who'd intended to help as a pilot, instead coordinated the many flights necessary to bring in guests from surrounding villages. Those living in villages 45 to 90 minutes away were picked up the day before, on Saturday.

Soon after the first planeload of guests arrived, Jeanne heard guitar music coming from upstairs in the lodge. Her heart leaped as she listened to men singing God's praise as they practiced for the memorial service. When the Penz children had been growing up in Alaska's bush, it had been rare to have believing Native men in their Sunday services. Now the men were not only present, but also providing the music—the fulfillment of many prayers.

By Sunday, word had spread in the villages about the memorial service. More and more people asked to come. Pilots kept loading up and flying them to Kako. The time set for the service had to be moved back an hour and a half before the guests had joined the family and staff—over 100 people total.

So many people wanted to share memories when given the opportunity that the planned two-hour service stretched out to over four hours. Jeanne wrote some memories from the testimonial part of the service and sent them to those who weren't able to attend:

- James, an older Eskimo man who was one of the guitar players and singers, told how Dave had led him to the Lord and that God had changed his life completely, even taking away his thirst for alcohol.
- George Landlord, an Eskimo pastor, shared how Dave had mentored and discipled him while he was on staff at Kako for eight years. Dave had encouraged him to reach out to the nearby village of Marshall for Bible studies, which eventually led to the starting of a church. It was men from that church who provided music for the service. Shortly before Dave passed away, he'd encouraged George to start reaching out to the next closest village. George made plans to do that.
- Clifford shared how Dave had talked to him about the Lord so often, he just wanted Dave to stop. But eventually, the

young man began to listen, turned to God, and expressed deep gratitude that Dave hadn't given up on him.

- Spencer, a gold miner, explained how Dave prayed for years until Spencer finally came to the Lord. (Jeanne noted how exciting that was. She had given up, but her parents hadn't.)

- Among those at the service, there was a definite consensus that being at Kako and spending time with Dave and Vera had been spiritually and relationally important for many.

Going on without Dave

When all the guests and family had returned home, only Bill and Brenda Johnson and eight-year-old Russell, their foster son, remained at the retreat center, along with Debbie, who'd been there through Dave's illness and stayed on for another couple of weeks. For the most part, Vera was alone with her memories and her grieving.

By June 24, Debbie had returned to her home in Washington State. Camp sessions for youth were going on, but Debbie wrote that her mother was "consumed with catching up on paperwork as well as taking on a lot of questions and decisions that Dave used to do." Jonathan was filling in for his father as acting interim director, but he had to be at his job in Bethel much of the time. Vera worked with a lawyer in settling Dave's estate while she negotiated an emergency loan from the bank to pay for aviation fuel, diesel, and propane arriving on the summer barge. Two vacancies needed to be filled on KRC's board, and those changes affected the account and the specifics needed for the bank to approve the loan. "All this weighs on her," Debbie wrote. "I am amazed at all she has to do and handle in the midst of grief."

As she'd done her whole life, Vera looked to the Lord not only for strength, but also for joy. A month after Dave's passing, she quoted author M. B. Anderson: "God confidently assures us—in the great symphony of life, the final refrain for the believing heart is triumphant, everlasting joy." And her communications from this period showed that she was resting in God's capable arms "as he leads us and carries us through these difficult days and the adjustments" they bring.

Carrying on with Summer Camps

Before Dave became so ill, the Rodkeys had already planned a trip to Kako to help with family camp. That's how they were on hand to help instead with the funeral, then the memorial service on the weekend originally planned for family camp. Jeanne wrote:

> It's a time of critical need. There is no one in place to take Dad's leadership role. Our family and the Kako staff are scrambling to put together a plan that allows the summer camp schedule to proceed. Camps for children start in the first week of June and go for six weeks. Gas costs for flying the planes continue to be high and promise to go much higher. And yet, the need for a "lighthouse" in the Y-K Delta of Western Alaska couldn't be greater. These camps and the ongoing relationships are important for sharing God's love and care for the people of the Delta.

God did send cabin leaders and all the other volunteers needed, including pilots from MATA, and camps went on as planned. "Miss Becky," who'd spent several summers working at Kako before and after marrying fellow worker John Erickson, gave up her summer to return. She became an invaluable help in carrying on the camps. John came for a week to construct a new water slide at the pond and helped set up activities for camp sessions.

The camps went well, but fatigue from back-to-back sessions began to wear on the staff. Many of them got sick during the next to the last week. By the final week of camp, Becky admitted she was tired and ready for a break from responsibility. But she kept in mind the homes the campers came from and the hope the staffers offered them. She said,

It is helpful for me to know where they are coming from, especially when they are pushing all my buttons and trying every angle to get their way and wear me down. It's helpful to know that B. lost her Mom to cancer and her Dad drowned this year. It's also helpful to know that her friend's parents are alcoholics and that S. was bumped from last week's camp to this week because they were having her Gram's funeral. Jesus understands weariness. The disciples must have been weary when Jesus asked them to labor with him in prayer. They fell asleep. I'm trying not to fall asleep on this last group of kids.

Becky was able to persist until all of the children returned home. She and the other volunteers took satisfaction in knowing that although Dave was not there to direct, God had seen to it that his life-changing Word and love went out to over 100 village kids. The reward would be seen in lives changed for eternity.

An Ongoing Story

With God's help, visionary David Carlton Penz laid an excellent foundation for the development of Kako, this "light in the wilderness." Jeanne summarized it well at her father's funeral service:

> *It just so happened* (a favorite saying of my mom's) that Dad had been in the Army and on his way to Korea when his ship received a message requesting some men to come to Alaska instead, and Dad responded.
>
> Then he *just so happened* to attend a good church in Anchorage that God helped him find—The Church of the Open Door.
>
> While attending there, *it just so happened* that he heard about a need for men to help build a chapel in an Indian village about 200 miles north of Anchorage,

and *it just so happened* that he was granted leave from the Army to go to help, and while there, felt God call him to come back to Alaska as a missionary. And then, when he and our family returned to Alaska as missionaries, *it just so happened* that the mission placed us at that same village where he had helped build the church. All of these *happenings* show me how God led him all along the way to work in Alaska.

The founding of Kako had also been part of God's leading.

Jeanne concluded her remarks with, "*It just so happened* that Dad learned about this gold mine."

That story, of course, is told in this book, and the story is not Dave's alone. It also belongs to Jan and their children. It's a story shared by dozens of other missionaries in other parts of Alaska. Hundreds of volunteers over the years have had an active part in it, as have the friends who supported it financially. It's the story of the people of the Yukon-Kuskokwim Delta who are hearing God's Word, turning to him for redemption from sin, and becoming part of God's worldwide Church.

It is equally Vera's story.

It was not coincidence that she was raised by a godly mother and chose to attend a Bible college where she heard and responded to the need of the Alaska's Native peoples.

Neither was it coincidence that she sat in class next to a young man who needed help with his grammar, nor that he also heard the call to Alaska.

It was not coincidence that after she experienced tragedy and perseverance and a life lived in service to others, God led her to join her life with a man whose love for Native people was as strong as hers.

Her life experiences had prepared her perfectly to spend 26 years in partnership with David Penz, building a lighthouse in the wilderness called Kako Retreat Center.

"Dave's death has left a huge hole," Vera wrote to her friends. "Someone has said it will take three people to fill his shoes. But nothing is too hard for God. We are trusting God to fill these holes just as he used Dave to start the work at Kako." Then this intrepid woman—small in stature but great in faith—added, "My heart's desire is to stay at Kako and be a part of the ongoing ministry as long as I am able."

CHAPTER 24
The First Summer without Dave Penz

Following the triumphant memorial service for Dave, his 46-year-old son Jonathan stepped smoothly into the role of acting director. He had come to Kako with his parents when he was 12 and lived there until his late 20s, working alongside his dad in every aspect of the operational needs.

Dave had also been 46 when he'd first taken on the Kako vision in 1978. When he became ill with leukemia in 2007, Jonathan returned and donated his time and expertise as a pilot and mechanic for nine months each year, taking work elsewhere for the remaining three months to support himself. Because he knew the people in the surrounding villages, understood Native culture, and shared his dad's vision for the retreat center, Jonathan was uniquely qualified for his new role. His wife, Sharon, had worked on staff at Kako before she married Jonathan and loved working with children and reaching out to village people.

Bill and Brenda Johnson remained on staff for a time, helping things to run smoothly. God provided staff, counselors, and pilots for that summer's camping program. The staff also included Becky and John Erickson. Vera carried the huge tasks of the bookwork, income tax, and settling the estate. She looked forward to later visiting and sharing in the villages.

Kyle Stevens, who had directed camp for several summers in the past, did not return that summer because he was preparing to marry Ella Townsend in August. His brother Andrew, who had also served at Kako, married Ella's sister Samantha on the same day.

Changes and Challenges

On November 4, 2014, Kako's residents traveled to Russian Mission to vote. Russian Mission had previously been a "dry" village, where possessing alcohol was legal, although selling it was not. In this election, a margin of five votes turned the village "damp." At the same time, marijuana became legal statewide. People at Kako wondered what would happen to believers with the additional temptations now facing them.

The next March, when Russian Mission and Fairbanks had a student exchange, all the kids came to Kako for two days of fun and learning. Sandra K., a matriarch from Russian Mission, accompanied them and taught the kids how to make akutaq (Eskimo ice cream). When she stayed at Vera's home, she told how the new alcohol regulations were affecting the village. She said that when the first shipment of 40 orders of booze arrived, some people carried on riotous revelry all night. Children sought refuge in her home because their parents were drunk. Sandra said her floor was wall to wall with children afraid to go home to sleep.

As 2015 began, the Kako board met in Anchorage and officially appointed Jonathan as KRC's Chief Executive Officer. Kyle Stevens brought his bride for a week's stay in February. He and Ella both returned to work full time that summer.

Then Kako's aging sewer and water systems brought challenges. The retreat center's water came from the dammed-up creek that flowed through the camp, along with a small well supplying only the Penzes' house, lodge, and washhouse. Now the Alaska Department of Environmental Conservation (DEC) required a new well for drinking water.

After weeks of working on their ancient well-drilling rig, Jonathan finally got it running, but the engine billowed smoke, revealing a cracked cylinder head. They couldn't start digging the new well after all. The eight houses would have to use creek water (if the DEC approved). The first week of camp had to be canceled, but temporary permits came through in time for the second week, and the summer season was a success.

In the fall, after freeze-up, Jonathan and helpers replaced the sewer line/drain field along the runway.

At the January 2016 board meeting, Kyle and Ella Stevens, with their new daughter Kate, were accepted as full-time staff. Then on January 14, baby Merrick was born to Jonathan and Sharon Penz. Work continued with getting the water and sewer systems up to code and developing plans for upgrades.

Jonathan wrote, "I am pleased that staff in the Alaska Department of Environmental Conservation appear to recognize not only the importance of protecting our people and the environment, but also the very real constraints of operating a camping ministry at a remote site in rural Alaska. We are working with them on practical solutions that meet the requirements of the law while still allowing Kako to operate this summer."

As had happened the previous year, they were given water permits for the lodge. They planned to install a water treatment plant to treat creek water for use in the other houses. The season began with one of the biggest gatherings ever for family camp over Memorial weekend when 113 village people were flown in. Native New Life Fellowship from Anchorage led the meetings. Many marriages were healed or strengthened that weekend.

Wildfire

Kids' camps were to begin on June 13. On June 3, lightning started a wildfire that burned in all directions, charring 23,000 acres. A call went out: pray for rain!

The fire burned to within seven miles of Kako. A 20-man crew came to cut brush around Kako, hoping to protect the buildings, but they could do nothing to protect the forest. Losing the black spruce and other trees would have been a huge loss. Campers loved Kako's trees, as many of the villages had only tundra.

The fire chief had pulled airplanes from the battle. Then rain began to fall, and he sent the water bombers back for a day. The combination of planes and rainfall brought the fire under control. To much rejoicing, the threat ended.

The Stevens family arrived with their belongings, and camp began on time. That year, 260 summer campers enjoyed the sessions, including John Erickson's new addition to camp fun. He constructed a 300-foot zip line to take kids soaring over a pond.

Each week on the last night of camp, Native pastor George Landlord shared his own faith and told the kids how much God loved them. He showed them that faith in God was not just a "white man's religion" but was for everybody, and the kids responded.

Time to Retire

By January 2017, Vera was thinking back on her 28 years of work at Kako. She realized that after serving for more than 60 years in Alaska and having reached the age of 86, she was ready to retire.

During her December visits to Debbie in Washington State, they had visited Hank and Joan Husby in their home at Warm Beach Senior Community. Vera reserved a lovely apartment at Warm Beach, and on February 28, 2017, tendered a letter of resignation to Kako's board. She would remain on staff as ambassador and consultant, but would move to Warm Beach after the coming busy summer season.

A Memorable Summer

In February, the Troyer family—John, Kat, and little Abel—returned to Kako. Kyle and Ella's new baby, Lauren, arrived ahead of time on March 20, weighing only 4 pounds.

In May, Lance Cramer, an Inupiaq from Kotzebue, along with his wife Corina and their children, worked with staff to put on one of the most blessed family camp events in memory. During one session, Jonathan was sitting up front, making the camp-wide speaker phone work in broadcast mode. People outside on the grounds heard Lance's animated storytelling and his hearers' laughter. Smiling, they came up the stairs to join the group and were also touched by the truths of God's Word.

Jonathan wrote, "By the final night we were a family. Over 115 of us. The last session went till midnight. No one wanted the retreat to be over. The faces I saw were locked on hope, serious and filled with hunger. Faith rising like a flood. Not toward the one who carried the message, but toward the one who brings life! The Lord showed his love in a tangible way that weekend, and the comfort he bestowed soothed many layers of hurt. People found a safe place to grieve, to mend, and to grow in strength. Praise be to God!"

Then it was again time for kids' camps, also blessed by God. When the six weeks concluded on July 14, beloved camp director Kyle Stevens shared this:

It is exciting as some campers hear the gospel for the first time...We see their faces and hear their questions as they learn about true forgiveness of sins, a life of victory and freedom in Christ, rather than a life strangled by the grip of sin. We saw the seed of the gospel fall on all types of ground, and we are rejoicing with those who had it take root and gave their lives to the Lord. Nothing can match the joy felt when you see the face of a young person who has just experienced God's saving grace.

While it is impossible to use hard numbers to gauge the work of the Holy Spirit in the 243 campers who attended this summer, we rejoice that we saw over 50 campers pray to receive Christ! We are confident that the seed planted in the others will not be easily forgotten, as the Word of God that was preached continues to work in their hearts and minds . . .

Later, in the nearer towns, we get to hear the children ask about their counselors and summer staff. Some kids look forward every day to possibly seeing them next summer here at Kako. While we work hard to make their camp experience as much fun as it can be, what really lasts in the campers' memories are the faces and names of the people who showed them true love and attention, in a place where they felt safe and secure. It is hard to see their tears as they leave and [it is hard] to tell them they can't stay, but we rejoice in the opportunity, and we are grateful that the Lord is using our supporters, summer staff and full-time staff to advance his kingdom here in the Y-K Delta.

Kyle asked for prayer as they planned ways to disciple the new Christians at home in their villages over the winter. "The spread of the true life-changing power of the gospel is not hindered by closed doors or hearts, but by so few missionaries and resources to reach out," he said.

A Special Berry Picking Retreat

August brought a very special berry picking retreat for women from 12 villages. Speaker Carolyn Lyman captured the attention of the 45 women when she told the story that had begun 33 years earlier.

She had been a believer, determined to serve the Lord. After she married her husband Spencer, a non-believing miner at Snow Gulch, her life was exciting and adventurous, but she didn't live wholeheartedly for God. Deep down she missed the joy of God's presence. One day, while her husband was away doing errands, she prayed desperately to find her way back to the Lord. She longed for someone to pray with her. Maybe that would help bring her close to the Lord again!

Then she heard the drone of a plane in the distance. Every passing plane in that lonely country was of interest, so she stepped outside to search the sky for it.

Dave Penz, in his Cessna 180, crested the hills and banked to view the Snow Gulch settlement below. *The Lyman's plane is gone. They must be out*, Dave thought. Then he saw Carolyn waving. People waving at a plane overhead was not unusual. Besides, a Christian should avoid any appearance of evil. Why then did he feel so strongly he should land?

As he brought the plane to a stop on the tiny runway, Carolyn ran up, weeping. "Oh, Dave, I was praying you would land! I'm tired of feeling like I'm running from God. Would you pray with me?"

Dave prayed, claiming with her 1 John 1:9 (KJV): "If we confess our sins, he is faithful and just to forgive us our sins, and to cleanse us from all unrighteousness."

As she repeated the words, she felt her life turn around. She was eager to tell others, especially her husband, about her faith.

Thirty-three years later, Carolyn stood in front of those 45 women and told of the power of holding onto God's promises and believing for his timing, touch, and forgiveness in our lives. She told of lessons learned during the nine years she prayed her husband would come to the Lord, and of his eventual salvation. The women responded with rapt attention. They went home encouraged, and at least one confessed her new life in Christ.

Jeanne Rodkey, there as a volunteer, wrote:

> So what does Ladies' Retreat do for these women? It's a place of peace in the midst of distressing life situations. It's a place for healing from hurts suffered. It's a place of connection, for meeting old friends who live in other villages, and a place to make new friends. It's a place to sing hymns together and hear teaching from God's Word. And hear from another woman how

God reached out to help her, which gives hope. It's a place where they can get back on track in their relationship with God and their families.

Before the end of that retreat, Vera shared thoughts about her 29 years at Kako, and with laughter, tears, and singing, the women showed appreciation to their friend. Then, with Debbie's help, Vera finished preparations for her move, and by September 2017 had settled into her new home at Warm Beach Senior Center.

A Winter of Tragedy

As October rains pelted Kako, spirits were still high from the spiritual advances made during the summer. Then unexpected disaster struck. The 36-year-old culvert—that supported the road connecting the airstrip to the camp complex—failed. Water escaping from the dammed-up pond washed out the berm and swept a shed and well house downstream. The flood damaged Kako's water system and left a huge gulley where the small creek usually ran.

Major repairs were needed. On Monday, October 16, Jonathan and Kyle left in separate planes, heading toward Bethel where they planned to pick up materials and volunteer helpers. They encountered heavy fog in the hills near Russian Mission, and large areas of fog elsewhere. Jonathan gained altitude to fly above the fog. Kyle was flying about 10 minutes behind him. The two spoke by radio about the weather, and Kyle said he was doing fine.

But Kyle did not arrive at Bethel. Had he had trouble and turned back? Jonathan picked up his load of volunteers and returned to Kako, watching for the missing Cessna 205 along the way. But Kyle was not at Kako.

Jonathan notified Alaska State Troopers of the missing pilot and plane, and the search began.

The next day, a boater on the Yukon River spotted wreckage sticking out of the water. It was towed to the bank and determined to be part of the missing plane. Alaska State Troopers used a boat-mounted SONAR device to locate the remaining portion of the plane under 20 feet of water. On Friday they recovered Kyle's body. Both Kyle's and Ella's parents flew to Kako to help and comfort Ella.

John Rodkey wrote in tribute:

> Kyle was an extraordinary person. Full of life, love, and energy, he had a kind and encouraging word for everyone. He was the kind of guy that any kid would love to have as an older brother, and kids up and down the Yukon and Kuskokwim, throughout the Delta area, looked up to him and looked forward to each new year of summer camps at Kako with him at the helm. Nothing gave him more joy than sharing how much Jesus meant to him and seeing Jesus make a difference in the lives around him.

Ella and the children returned to California to live with family. Jonathan and Sharon were left to deal with their own grief as well as damage to the water system and other ongoing problems. Winter brought weeks of 30-below-zero temperatures and more than five feet of snow. Volunteers cut wood and kept fires burning. Jonathan kept equipment going to plow snow and haul wood.

The ministry at Kako felt the loss of their friend in many ways. Jonathan wondered how they would ever find another full-time camp director who would live at Kako and have the same heart for people that Kyle had demonstrated.

But then John and Becky Erickson, who lived in Fairbanks but had spent many summers working at Kako, agreed to oversee the camping program and its staffing for the coming summer. Jonathan felt reassured that this was just the latest in God's provision for Kako's leadership.

When Ed Hooley's dream of a retreat center at Kako seemed blocked, God had already prepared Dave's heart to carry on the task. When Jan passed away, God brought Vera, a woman well suited for the challenge. God responded faithfully to the prayers of warriors around the country to build a place of refuge for the hungry hearts of Alaskan Natives. And when Dave finished his task, God had already prepared Jonathan to carry on his dad's work.

Chapter 25
Life at Kako

Life in a remote spot like Kako means living with what the climate dishes out. Short summers have long hours of daylight. Days can be mild and sunny, or there can be long periods of rain. The warm Japanese current flowing along the coast influences the climate in this part of Alaska. Moisture-laden clouds drift over the Interior to drop their loads as rain in the summer and as snow in the dark, cold winters.

On summer days when the air is still, swarms of mosquitoes drill for blood from any warm-blooded creature available. When the mosquitoes die off, black gnats, no-see-ums and white-sox bite and pester. Like all rural Alaskans, people at Kako cover up, use repellants, and keep on working.

In addition to heavy snow, winter also brings fog, wind, and bone-chilling cold. But whatever the weather, work is always waiting to be done at Kako. Fires have to be kept burning in all the residences during cold weather, whether or not they are occupied, so frost will not push basement walls in and freeze and burst the water pipes. In order to keep the fires burning, someone has to first cut, limb, and haul in logs, then split and store the wood at each house. Volunteers are needed each year, not only to bring in logs for firewood, but also to make lumber.

Energy Needs
Kako uses a diesel generator to produce its own electricity.

Keeping the generator in operating order is a priority. To save on fuel, the generator runs only part-time, from 8:00 a.m. until 1:00 p.m. and again in the evenings from 4:00 to 10:00 p.m. Work that requires electricity has to be done during those times.

Diesel fuel to heat the lodge and to run the generator and heavy equipment is expensive. Crude oil comes by pipeline from North Slope oil fields to the refinery at North Pole. From there it is transported by truck to Nenana, then down the Yukon by barge. This is how aviation gas (avgas) needed for the airplanes, snow machines, and four wheelers is transported too. The barge also brings propane in 180-pound tanks for cookstoves and water heaters. Fuel must be paid for upon delivery, and the bill runs into tens of thousands of dollars each summer. The alternative is buying fuel as needed in the villages, which is much more costly.

Barge operators unload diesel and avgas into Kako's big tanks on the Yukon's shore near Kako Lake. There are three 5,000-gallon tanks. Two hold diesel, the other avgas. When needed, fuel is transferred into two 500-gallon tanks that are dragged on a sled behind the Caterpillar to the retreat center. The trip takes five to six hours if all goes well—longer when frequent stops must be made to cool the engine or drain water out of the fuel system. Propane cylinders are hauled by sled behind a four-wheeler in summer and by snow machine in winter.

Transportation for Kako

Transportation for Kako Retreat Center has been the subject of frequent prayer requests. Small planes need constant maintenance or repairs. They fly uncounted miles across some of the wildest, loneliest places on earth and must be kept in top condition. If a plane is out of commission for a while, replacements have to be borrowed or rented. And of course, pilots are needed to do the flying. At times there haven't been enough planes or pilots available for all the people who'd like to come to a camp session or retreat.

When the planes are outside in winter, nylon covers, like big insulated blankets, surround the planes' engine cowlings to protect them. Electric heaters are used inside the covers. On the bottoms of the oil pans, heaters similar to hot pads are used. Head-bolt heaters, with bands that fit around the cylinders of the engine, keep the cylinders warm.

Some years ago pilots used catalytic heaters to warm aircraft cabins before flying, but now most people use electric heaters for that purpose. If Kako people go to a village for an overnight stay, they just stow the insulated covers and heaters in the back of the plane. Then they can plug them in to warm the plane before leaving. Keeping planes warm can be a problem, though, when flying to places that don't have electricity.

Maintenance of the airstrip itself will be easier once crews put drainage tiles in place beneath the runway. Presently, water accumulating in the ground freezes and expands during the winter. This causes frost boils that thaw in the spring, then collapse, making dangerous soft spots. The bucket loader is used to fill in sunken spots. Then the grader scrapes the surface smooth again.

For onsite transportation, four-wheelers are used in summer and snow machines in winter. The missionaries can scavenge broken-down machines for replacement parts. It takes about three no-longer-usable four-wheelers to provide parts to keep one running. In summer, at least four operational vehicles are needed to haul people and materials around camp and between KRC and Kako Landing on the river. For winter use, Dave developed a simple but tough type of sled to pull behind a snow machine—the Kako version of a pickup truck. These sleds proved to be so useful that Dave and helpers made more of them to sell for use in the villages. The villagers arrived by snow machine and hauled them home, causing the sleds to become another source of income for the center.

Daily Needs

Those living at Kako provide much of their own food. Like

their neighbors in the villages, people at Kako depend largely upon wild game for meat. They catch salmon and other fish in the Yukon. They drive four-wheelers six miles over the rough, muddy trail to Kako Lake, then canoe a quarter-mile across the lake to cast among the grasses for pike. In winter, they can make a hole in the ice to catch pike and other fish. They usually shoot their moose in December, fill the freezers, and have enough to share. Occasionally they add beaver or bear meat to the freezers. Black bears frequently wander into the center, and sometimes they became part of the groceries.

Feeding people who come to Kako is a big job. Staples have to be ordered ahead and flown into Russian Mission, then into Kako. On top of everything else that goes on during the short summers, the Penzes and staff plant a garden from which they harvest root vegetables for the winter. They also grow lettuce and other fresh veggies for summer treats and the freezer. In both greenhouse and garden, Vera at times grew flowers, even roses, that she shared with people from the villages. She picked and froze wild berries as well.

Livestock and Wild Creatures

Fresh eggs come from Kako's chickens, which must be fed, housed, kept warm, and protected from predators. At first, the Penzes tried letting their chickens run free, but soon hawks discovered the poultry and began swooping down and carrying them off. Then the Penzes tried a pen covered with fish netting, but the hawks figured out how to get through the spaces in the netting, and they'd kill and eat the chickens right there. Ermines (northern weasels) were a problem too. One night they killed fifty young chickens. So Dave built a chicken coop, and now the birds live inside.

Once they even raised turkeys. One morning Dave walked down to his plane and saw a turkey roosting on each wingtip and a third on the cowling behind the propeller. He didn't get a picture, because as soon as they saw him, they came flying to him for a handout.

The Penzes considered raising goats for their milk. A friend offered them seven baby miniature goats, but no one could be available on a daily basis to milk and care for them. They'd have needed a shed and a sturdy fence, too, because goats climb everywhere. Another friend raised goats, but had a struggle keeping them penned in. One morning he came out to his airplane to find that one of the animals had hopped up on the tail and trotted to the cockpit. Its legs had poked through the fabric and were hanging down inside the airplane. The friend told Dave, "The goat was bleating, 'Baa, baa! Get me out of here!'"

Domestic animals are always subject to predators. Coyotes have only recently arrived in this part of Alaska. Occasionally wolves come around. Once the Penzes had a pet dog that they kept inside. They heard wolves howling around the house. The dog went wild, frantic to get out. Dave took his gun and opened the door, intending to slip out and scare them away. But the dog pushed its way past before Dave could grab it and rushed toward the wolves. They never saw the dog again.

Humans can also find themselves in danger from wild animals, although animals prefer to avoid humans. Once, while Dave and four other men were working near the shop, they noticed a big brown bear meandering up the runway toward them. When the bear smelled and saw them, it leaped sideways through the air and barreled into the woods. The men later measured seventeen feet between the last set of footprints on the runway and the spot where the bear landed.

Another time, from the air, Dave spotted a brown bear "riding" a moose. The desperate moose could not shake the bear off, so Dave flew lower, trying to scare the bear. It did let go, but didn't run away. The moose was too weak to struggle anymore, and Dave knew the bear would kill it. Over a period of ten days, when Dave flew to Russian Mission to get the mail, he'd see the bear eating its fill, then sleeping nearby, guarding his catch. Finally he'd had enough to eat, and raked brush over the carcass to hide it. Waiting scavengers finished it off.

CHAPTER 26
What Does It Take to Reach a Village?

Imagine a circle 320 miles in diameter dropped over the hills, rivers and boggy lowlands of the vast Yukon-Kuskokwim Delta. Its edge extends westward to the waters of the Bering Sea, and to the Kuskokwim Mountains on the south and east. Scattered over the wild terrain along the waterways and seacoast are more than 50 villages. Some are home to only a few families. Others are large enough to be called towns. Some residents are Athabascan Indian, Caucasian, or other races. Most people in the villages within Kako's radius of service are Yupik Eskimo—short, stocky people well adapted to their harsh climate. The town of Russian Mission, on the Yukon River only a short distance from Kako, marks the general line of division between the Eskimo population to the west and Athabascan to the east.

In those more than 50 settlements, the population totals only 25,000 or so. That's hardly enough to make a small city in the other 49 states. Why would a couple like Dave and Vera Penz leave the comfort of friends and family to spend their lives reaching out to such a small number of people in the Alaska wilderness?

For Kako's leaders and the many supporters and volunteers who assist them, it's the commission Jesus spoke in Scripture: "You shall be My witnesses both in Jerusalem, and in all Judea and Samaria, and even to the remotest part of the earth" (Acts 1:8 NASB). Alaskan volunteers leave their own towns (their Jerusalems) to go into the Judea of more distant parts of Alaska, such as the Yukon-Kuskokwim Delta. For those who come from the other 49 states, Kako can seem like the most remote part of the earth. But its people are precious to the Lord. That makes the effort all worthwhile.

The People

What are the Yupiks like? Outsiders usually find these people to be reserved until they are sure of a newcomer's trustworthiness. Then they can become faithful friends. Native people have a dry sense of humor. They are generally nonaggressive, self-effacing, and gentle of speech. But they can also be critical and intolerant of fellow villagers who go outside of cultural norms.

In their early ministries, Dave and Jan Penz, as well as Vera and Al Kelley, learned how difficult it can be to share Christ with their Native neighbors.

Some Natives are superstitious, influenced by entrenched cultural beliefs. Because outsiders have taken advantage of them, they find it hard to trust newcomers. In one village, a local storekeeper was so suspicious, thinking that Dave planned to rip them off, he would spit on the ground whenever he saw him. Dave continued to be friendly. That was more than 30 years ago. Eventually the man asked if his children could come to camp, and his attitude changed completely. He saw that the Penzes had been trying to help the Natives all along, and now he goes out of his way to help Kako.

Native people are isolated from the rest of the world because their villages are usually located in roadless country. Often in many villages, one family wields most of the power and control. It's difficult to make a positive change if the controlling family doesn't agree with the change. Villagers can come down hard on people who aren't part of the power complex. If someone becomes an evangelical believer, he or she goes outside the norm and can expect to be isolated and ostracized because of it. This once was especially true if the village was mainly Catholic or Russian

Orthodox, because the church leaders did not want to lose their members.

Alcoholism and drug addictions are part of the legacy of outside cultures. As happened to Native Americans in the Lower 48, Alaska's Native peoples not only have been affected by alcohol and drugs and the physical and mental abuse that comes with these addictions, but they also face a welfare mentality, limited opportunities caused by isolation, cultural breakdown, difficult travel, poverty, and prejudice from the larger culture.

Violence, Abuse, Suicide

Village life doesn't always offer the idyllic, peaceful existence that one might imagine, although the months of June and July bring busy, happy times for many villagers. That's when salmon are running in the rivers and families work hard at their fish camps, drying fish for the winter. At other times, villages can become noisy places, with drunken screaming and fighting at all hours of the night and snow machines roaring up and down the streets. Kako Retreat Center offers a quiet place where people can rest, away from the turmoil.

A village can also be a place of violence, especially in homes where one or both parents are alcoholic. Children grow up in abuse, with low expectations for themselves and others. In many communities, half of the boys have been sexually abused. Almost every girl and woman—90 percent by some estimates—has experienced sexual abuse. When young girls are raped, sometimes by trusted members of the extended family, these girls can become suicidal. Men and boys are even more likely than females to consider suicide as an easy way out of their troubles.[14]

14 "As of 2010, Alaska has the nation's second-highest suicide rate, according to the Centers for Disease Control. Only Wyoming, with a suicide rate of 23.2 suicides for every 100,000 people, had a higher rate than Alaska's 23.1 per 100,000 people, according to the CDC. Alaska's suicide rate for the 2003-2011 period was 21.6 per 100,000 people, compared to a national average of 11.3 per 100,000 for the period, CDC records say."

LIVING GOLD

When Jeanne Penz Rodkey talked at the 2013 Ladies' Berry Picking Retreat about her mother's suicide, her words resonated with her listeners. One strong Christian woman attended the conference three weeks after she'd lost her son to suicide. Her grief was overwhelming. All she could say was, "Why didn't he talk to me?" A young girl from the village of Hooper Bay, which has a particularly high rate of such deaths, admitted to Jeanne that she had often struggled with thoughts of suicide. Then a friend killed herself. At her friend's funeral, she watched the friend's young cousin shaking the body, calling her cousin's name and crying, "Wake up! Wake up!" The first girl decided she could never do that to another small child and changed her mind about suicide.

Substance Abuse

At the same retreat, a concerned woman spoke up about what she had learned concerning village kids abusing Internet-accessible prescription drugs. "Go home and bring the problem to your village and regional councils," she urged the others.

She explained that drugs are easily available via the Internet without a prescription. The only thing teens need to do to have the drugs delivered to their village post offices is give a debit-card number. Unaware of the terrible side effects, such as seizures that can lead to heart stoppage, kids as young as elementary age are experimenting to get high. Some have died. Others must be hospitalized and weaned off the drugs slowly.

Susan Foster, M.S.W., vice president and director of Policy Research and Analysis at CASA Columbia, confirms what the village women discussed. She wrote, "The Internet serves as an

Yereth Rosen, "Study: Suicide rates increase as Alaska community sizes get smaller, farther north," Anchorage *Daily News*, November 16, 2013, updated May 31, 2016, accessed June 28, 2018, https://www.adn.com/rural-alaska/article/high-latitudes-small-populations-correlated-alaska-suicide-prevalance/2013/11/17.

open channel for distribution of controlled prescription drugs with no mechanisms to even block sales to children."[15]

Drug use by kids has now replaced alcoholism, which was the main problem 20 years ago. According to recent statistics, among ages 12 and up, Alaska ranks the highest in the percentage of illegal drug use in the United States—13.5 percent.[16]

John Rodkey observes, "There is a very deep, palpable and rending grief that rips and grips the Native population. A seemingly unending and unstoppable cycle of alcoholism and drug abuse, sexual abuse, violence, and suicide results in a culture where most people are not through grieving the most recent death before the next one happens. Masking their pain with alcohol (or drugs) only results in additional tragic events." John adds, "We have seen that where the grace of Christ comes into the life of a few members of a small village, the cycle can be slowed or stopped, but it is the work of decades, not years; of generations, not moments."

Respecting the Village Culture

Many Natives have found that once they "hit the road system," they change their whole lifestyle. They want cars, television sets, and all the things that city people have. To acquire those things, they must get steady jobs. They are no longer satisfied in the village. If they do try to come back to live in the village, people there make fun of them because they have changed. They've lost their roots and don't stay.

A few Bible schools were founded to train Native Alaska students, including Alaska Christian College in Soldotna, Alaska

---

15 Sue McGreevey, "Use, Abuse of Internet Pharmacies," *The Harvard Gazette*, December 19, 2011, accessed June 28, 2018, https://news.harvard.edu/gazette/story/2011/12/use-abuse-of-internet-pharmacies.

16 Table 14, National Survey on Drug Use and Health, 2013 and 2014, SAMHSA, Center for Behavioral Health Statistics and Quality, accessed July 2, 2018, https://www.samhsa.gov/data/sites/default/files/1/1/NSDUHsaeAlaska2014.pdf

Bible College in Glennallen (later moved to Palmer), and Alaska Bible Institute in Homer. But it's hard for the schools to attract and keep students from the bush for the reasons listed above. Instead, many non-Natives enroll, including some from the other 49 states who are eager to see Alaska inexpensively.

However, some Native students do get their training at these schools. Each year, for example, Homer's Alaska Bible Institute sends a work team, including Native students, to help at Kako.

Dave felt strongly that village students needed to attend school near where they lived. That way they wouldn't become "citified" and lose their culture. Kako is ideally situated as a sort of "halfway house" solution. Students can be taught in ways that take advantage of their innate abilities, and they can easily commute between Kako and their homes.

With excitement, he had plans drawn up for a facility to house the institute he visualized. The three-level, 50-x-100-foot building would have classrooms, a media center, a bookstore, offices, and a student lounge. The daylight basement would be used for homeschooling and kids' activities. Ten motel-type units for the students would occupy the top floor.

Crews moved three of the campers' cabins farther down the hill to make room for the planned building. They graded a site next to the washhouse-lodge complex. And then they waited for funds to complete it. And waited. The space dedicated to housing the Leadership Training Institute still sits empty, but classes were successfully held in Hooley Lodge for several years.

Two of the Native students in the first class, George and Eunice Landlord, came to live at Kako as resident students, accompanied by their little son. They stayed for several years, studying and ministering in the villages, eventually becoming associate staff members. George's gift for evangelism among his own people made his ministry very effective. During the Landlords' time at Kako, some of the white staff left for various reasons. Although they were missed, according to Vera, "One of the blessings in it was that the Native people who were here, like George and Eunice, took a more active role. When Native people came to the workshops and retreats, they'd gravitate to George and Eunice because the Landlords understood what they'd been through."

Those who attended leadership training classes were enthusiastic about their growing understanding of the Bible and their increasing faith. Some came to faith for the first time, and many went home eager to share what they had learned. In Mountain Village, men who had previously left the work of their local church to the women began to take on the leadership roles.

Tenacity

Occasionally, the Holy Spirit works in miraculous ways to bring large numbers to Christ. But often progress comes slowly. The Penzes and others often witnessed to individuals for years before they surrendered to Christ.

John Rodkey says that tenacity must be a prominent characteristic of anyone called to bring Christ to Alaska's Natives.

Tenacious certainly is the right word to describe Dave and Vera's pursuit of the Kako dream. Over the years, it took tenacity to carry out the retreat center's building program. The Penzes and their helpers worked hard to build relationships with villagers. As already described, they offered summer camps, retreats, and teaching sessions where villagers of all ages could come to know Jesus as their Savior and helper, and then to be discipled in the way of Christ.

Kako: A Safe Place

Vera's grandson Justin Holland spent six months helping at Kako. He wrote: "I can't count how many times I've met people who simply came to Kako for an escape [from the atrocities of village life]. There is something to be said about Kako as a safe haven, for many seek it out for sanctuary. I have met grown men and seen them weep as they told me how Dave was like a father to them and how he had changed their lives. Women have confided in me how Vera inspires them and awes them with her perseverance."

Little Is Much When God Is in It

Though the vast, sparsely populated Y-K Delta might seem scarcely worth bothering about, each of its human inhabitants is precious to God.

"Little Is Much When God Is in It," written in 1924 by Kittie Louise Suffield, could be Kako's theme song:

In the harvest field now ripened
There's a work for all to do;
Hark! The voice of God is calling
To the harvest calling you.

Does the place you're called to labor
Seem too small and little known?
It is great if God is in it,
And He'll not forget His own.

Are you laid aside from service,
Body worn from toil and care?
You can still be in the battle,
In the sacred place of prayer.

Because the Delta people are dear to his heart, God called not only Dave and Vera Penz to spend their lives in this neglected harvest field, but he also called and is still calling many others to help.

Chorus:
Little is much when God is in it!
Labor not for wealth or fame.
There's a crown—and you can win it,
If you go in Jesus' name.

Would you like to join in this good work? For more information about Kako and how you can be involved, go to kakoretreatcenter. org.

You can sign up to receive newsletters by emailing Jonathan Penz at jonopenz@gmail.com.

To give, donate online or by sending a check to Kako Retreat Center at Box 29, Russian Mission, AK 99657.

Jonathan, Merrick, and Sharon Penz
Credit: Kako Retreat Center

Kyle and Ella Stevens with Kate and Lauren
Credit: Kako Retreat Center

Rebecca and John Erickson
Credit: John and Rebecca Erickson

Appendix: Methods of Ground Sluicing and Drilling for Gold

Ground Sluicing

To do ground sluicing, workers constructed a 20-foot long, open-ended sluice box with cross-riffles along the bottom and set it in the creek. From either side of the upper end, they angled in a four-foot-high solid steel wall. Using a Caterpillar tractor, they pushed sand into the open, upper end of the box. Water washing through the box carried the lighter sand away, allowing the heavy gold to settle out behind the riffles. Only about 50 percent of the gold was recovered in this way. The rest remained in the waste, which the Cat pushed away from the lower end of the sluice box as it accumulated.

Placer gold comes from old deposits in higher country. As bits of gold weather out of the original deposit, they wash downhill. The precious metal accumulates in cracks and crevices along creek bottoms, just as it does in sluice boxes. Old creek beds are often covered with deep alluvial deposits (sand, silt, clay, gravel, and larger rocks) washed down by flowing water. If gold is present, it will be found below all this. To discover where a vein of gold lies, it is necessary to drill down through the deposits, or "overburden."

Drilling for Gold

When the Yukon Mining Company entered the area, it brought a team to drill out, or explore possibilities, in Kako Creek. The driller, Alex Mingo, drove sections of five-inch pipe at intervals across the bottom of the streambed. Every few feet, a "bailer" would be lowered into the mixture of mud, gravel, and water in the pipe. The bailer, with a one-way valve on the bottom, scooped out the mixture, which was then panned for gold and a count taken of the number of gold specks. Alex bored as far down as 50 feet until he reached bedrock and could drill no farther. He covered the width of the creek in that manner, searching for pay dirt.

Any gold present would be found where the overburden was deepest, with lesser amounts called "side pay" on either side of the pay streak. Since creek beds move back and forth over the years, sometimes the pay streak wasn't even beneath where the creek presently ran. If Alex found nothing in a cross section of creek, he'd move the drilling rig 50 feet upstream and try again. If he hit pay dirt, he'd drill on either side to see how wide the vein might be.

Once the Yukon Mining Company knew where gold was, it barged in machinery to remove the overburden and get at the pay dirt. In 1934, at a time of high water, a barge came up the Yukon River and nosed into shore a couple miles closer to Kako than was usually possible. It carried three big D7 Caterpillar tractors, a big dragline (a Northwest 80D), and a crane with a 100-foot boom. Clearing a road as they went, workers drove the machinery to the mine. The barge also carried machinery for a sawmill, lumber for camp buildings, and other needed equipment. They used a Cat and a stone boat (a sledge on runners) to drag all of this to the mining site.

The company hired workers to build the sawmill and then make lumber for a trestle sluice box. In constructing the sluice box, they built a long trestle, like a railroad bridge, and fashioned a box at the upper end, about 12 feet above ground level, into which the dragline dumped sand. A metal sluice box about three feet across, with two-foot sides, slanted 50 to 60 feet from the upper box down to the ground. A 10-inch pipe carried water to wash the sand through the sluice box. Large diesel-powered pumps recycled the water. As waste sand and gravel accumulated below the sluice box, the dragline picked up the waste and dumped it into tailings piles. Periodically, work stopped so the miners could remove the riffles and clean up the gold in the box.

Resources

Printed Resources:

Penz, Janet. *Where in the World Is Kako, Alaska? and What in the World Are David and Janet Penz Doing There???* Self-published,1981.

Crandall, Faye E. Crandall. *Into the Copper River Valley: The Letters and Ministry of Vincent James Joy, Pioneer Missionary to Alaska.* New York: Carlton Press, 1983.

Alaska Nuggets. Glennallen, Alaska: Central Alaska Missions.

Vera's newspaper clippings relating to her family's accident on Prince William Sound.

Prayer letters and other communications from Vera Kelley Penz over a period of more than fifty years.

Communications from Jeanne and John Rodkey and Jonathan Penz.

Missionary Aviation Training Academy newsletters (available on website below).

These online articles and websites were particularly valuable:

John Rodkey's adventures in bringing home a bear to Camp Inowak: http://mail.westmont.edu/pipermail/aeronca/2009-April/106622.html.

Kyle and Andrew Stevens at Kako: http://www.alotofstevens.com/2011/06/hello-from-alaska.html.

John and Rebecca Erickson's website: http://www.stellarflex.com/john.htm.

John Erickson on Kong Island camp: http://www.stellarflex.com/2ak09.htm.

Kako Retreat Center: www.kakoretreatcenter.org, http://www.heritageaflame.org/about-the-ministry/alaska-kako-retreat-center.

Missionary Aviation Training Academy (MATA) http://www.mata-usa.org.

Arctic Barnabas, an organization that encourages and supports missionaries in isolated communities http://arcticbarnabas.org.

Made in the USA
San Bernardino, CA
12 January 2019